Healing Paralysis

Copyright © 2006 Richard M. Lynch, PHD
All rights reserved.
ISBN: 0-9785750-0-8
Library of Congress Control Number: 2006906161

To order additional copies, please contact us.
BookSurge Publishing
www.booksurge.com
1-866-308-6235
orders@booksurge.com

Healing Paralysis

A Bible Primer For Rasheed and Others Desperately Seeking God

Richard M. Lynch, PHD

LFG Publishing
Riverside, NJ
2006

Healing Paralysis

TABLE OF CONTENTS

Acknowledgements xi

FOREWORD xvii

Chapter 1 – Introduction 1
    Foundations 7
    Health Beliefs: A Precursor to Healthy Decisions and
        Behaviors 14
    Who Should Consider This Book 18
    Quick Summary of Organization of the Holy Bible 21

Chapter 2 – Our Inheritance of Adam's Sin 23
    Genesis Chapter 1 23
    Genesis Chapter 2 27
    Genesis Chapter 3 31

Chapter 3 – The Prophecy of the Redeemer 35
    2 Samuel Chapter 7 36
    1 Chronicles Chapter 22 40
    Isaiah Chapter 7 43
    Isaiah Chapter 9 46
    Isaiah Chapter 53 49

Chapter 4 – God's Descent to Earth (in His own words) 53
    Matthew Chapter 5 55
    Matthew Chapter 7 59
    Matthew Chapter 9 62
    Matthew Chapter 12 65
    Matthew Chapter 16 69
    Matthew Chapter 24 72
    Matthew Chapter 28 76
    John Chapter 3 79

    John Chapter 5.. 82
    John Chapter 6.. 86
    John Chapter 14... 91
    John Chapter 16... 95
    John Chapter 17... 98
Chapter 5 – God's Ultimate Sacrifice – Himself................. 101
    Matthew Chapter 26... 103
    Matthew Chapter 28... 109
    Mark Chapter 15.. 112
    Mark Chapter 16.. 116
    Revelation Chapter 22....................................... 119

Chapter 6 – Jesus the Christ (According to Apostle Paul)........ 123
    Ephesians Chapter 3... 125
    Philippians Chapter 2....................................... 128
    Colossians Chapter 3.. 131
    I Timothy Chapter 3... 134
    Hebrews Chapter 1... 136

Chapter 7 – About Un-clean Meats............................... 139
    Genesis Chapter 1... 140
    Leviticus Chapter 10.. 143
    Leviticus Chapter 11.. 146
    Mark Chapter 7.. 150
    Acts Chapter 10... 154
    I Timothy Chapter 4... 158

Chapter 8 – Summary.. 161
    Summary Notes... 171

ACKNOWLEDGEMENTS

As I reflect on the visage of the men and women that I see suspending my bed through the opening in the roof, there are many who I wish to thank who knowingly or unknowingly contributed to the preparation of the book.

Andrea
I thank you for your demonstrated love, diligence, faith, temperance, patience and forgiveness; those very qualities which Paul instructed the followers of Christ to manifest as I came to accept Christ and as I continue to grow in Him. As faith is the substance of things hoped for, the evidence of things not seen, yours continues to manifest a power to transform and transcend.

Richard, Matthew & Langston
Thanks for your inestimable love, and for all you do to motivate and help me become the best man that I can be.

Rev. Drs. Abraham and Eve Fenton
Words can not express the gratitude that I have for your intelligent and thoughtful guidance that surely emanates from a lifetime of walking and working in Christ. To you and the senior leadership team at Abundant Life Fellowship, thank you for legitimizing my need to love the Lord with my mind as well as my heart and soul, and for galvanizing the word of God into the lives of my family and so many others.

Rev. Dr. DeForest "Buster" Soares, Jr
Thank you for your early example as a strong Christian man, and for allowing your strength to give me the confidence to open-up and express my questions about who Jesus is, as I was making my decision to accept Him or not. Thanks for not giving me the answers, but instead for validating my questions and directing me to where I could find the answers for myself.

Dr. & Mrs. Lester and Juanita Bynum

Your walk was the best evangelism that I could have received. You modeled intelligence, professionalism, success, confidence, integrity, family values, affluence and a service to Christ that was pivotal in shaping critical aspects of the man that I was becoming. Thanks for being who God intended, and for the love that you show our children as Godparents.

Rev. Joan and Edward Bullock

The friendship that you took the initiative to develop with us while at Shiloh Baptist Church and that we maintain over the years, always felt like a gift from God...a gift of a wiser older sister and brother. Thanks for being patient as I grew, and for seeing in me, something that I could not. Thanks for the Vineyard!

Rev. Dr. Arthur Jackson

Thanks for being the "light" in the family for you're your continued love and support.

Min. Michael Gray

Every man needs a good friend and brother in Christ. Thanks for your insights and for reminding me of the importance of keeping myself in it.

Thanks to the creators of www.crosswalk.com for making the text of the Authorized King James Version of the Holy Bible available in electronic format, which was used to import scripture references.

To my Parents,

My Brother and Sisters

and

my Loving Wife and Children

FOREWORD

Dr. Richard Lynch is one of those men blessed with a capacity to make a beneficial impact on the people among whom he lives and serves. He has demonstrated that in his capacity of a university professor, a successful entrepreneur, and leadership trainer. But nowhere is that more manifest than in his relationships to parents and his own immediate family.

Raised a Muslim, he became convinced of the case for Jesus, and is currently a dedicated believer and follower of Christ. Even though that created significant tensions it is refreshing to observe the respect and admiration that he has for his father and mother, and his gratitude for the sturdy upbringing which emphasized respect, diligence, learning, hard work, perseverance, self reliance, and much more. He credits that upbringing as being greatly responsible for his considerable achievements.

One can surely understand his burning desire to share his faith with his father and mother. Not only would that eliminate the greatest source of tension from their treasured relationship, but it would enable them to share the temporal and eternal benefits which he finds in his faith. One can also understand his desire for his children and their generation to embrace the ethic of respect, diligence, learning, hard work, perseverance, and self reliance, but also to embrace an intelligent and vibrant faith in Jesus.

That provides the driving force behind this book, *Healing Paralysis*. Rasheed is not only Dr. Lynch's father. In a manner of speaking he is representative of a much wider population of "Others Desperately Seeking God." Dr. Lynch sees them as seeking what Jesus offers, but they are hampered by serious misconceptions about Him. They do not understand who Jesus is, nor do they know what He said about Himself, or what the prophets said about Him. This book addresses these misconceptions, and diffuses many a difficult argument.

Healing Paralysis takes the reader on a journey of discovery so that the reader may have a more authentic understanding of Jesus and what He offers. It is a masterful work laying out the case for Jesus contextualized especially for those in Islam who really want to know about Jesus. It shows the need for respectful dialogue as opposed to verbal combat when discussing different views about God, and by extension everything else.

Healing Paralysis is practical and easy to follow especially when read as the author suggests.

Dr. Abraham E. Fenton
Founder, Abundant Life Fellowship.

CHAPTER I

Introduction

And it came to pass on a certain day, as he was teaching, that there were Pharisees and doctors of the law sitting by, which were come out of every town of Galilee, and Judaea, and Jerusalem: and the power of the Lord was present to heal them. And, behold, men brought in a bed a man which was taken with a palsy: and they sought means to bring him in, and to lay him before him. And when they could not find by what way they might bring him in because of the multitude, they went upon the housetop, and let him down through the tiling with his couch into the midst before Jesus. And when he saw their faith, he said unto him, *Man, thy sins are forgiven thee* (Luke 5:17-19).

The motivation for this book started last summer. My father had recently retired from his lifelong career as a carpenter and housing code inspector. He sold his New Jersey home, and purchased a smaller home in a relatively rural area of North Carolina. To assist him in preparing for the move, I planned go down to his new home in June and spend a few days helping him to paint and perform other repairs. In doing this I would also be sure to convey my sincere appreciation for him. This, I deeply wanted my dad to feel. I also knew that this time together would give us a chance to have a long-overdue one-on-one talk.

Why was this one-on-one needed? Earlier in the year, dad came to our home for a visit and said,

"Son, whenever we are here for dinner or a celebration we feel very comfortable and your home is very peaceful, however, lately, I've noticed that when you bless the food, you have us hold hands and always end your prayers with *in Jesus' name*. When you do that, it places those of us who are not Christians in an awkward position, as if we are in agreement that our prayers are going to Jesus. I would appreciate it if you would just end the prayer with *Amen but no Jesus*. If you are not comfortable with that, then let us know and those of us in the family who are not Christians can form our own circle and pray separately."

Dad fully expected that my response would be to honor his concerns and accommodate him by choosing the former option, which would certainly assure everyone's comfort...everyone's but mine!

"No dad. As much as I can understand your discomfort, and while it may be polite to make generic prayers in public places to accommodate a variety of faiths, in my home, we will worship the Lord in the name of Jesus! If you are uncomfortable with that, you may form your own prayer circle if you need to."

My sister who happened to be visiting at the time, and who had accepted Christ long ago, was rather surprised by the abrupt coldness and lack of deference apparent in my rejection of his request. My wife, on the other hand was happy that I "stood up" for what we believe in. For my part, I was quite conflicted. Conflicted because on one hand, I was offended that dad had the audacity to challenge me and my family on our religious beliefs in my house, while on the other, because I allowed that insult to distract me from proclaiming the greatest possible expression of the love which I have for my father. As I lay in bed that evening, I wished that I had told him the truth; that I loved him so much, that I wouldn't think of praying without invoking the name of Jesus, and thereby the Holy Spirit to bring peace to those for whom our prayers are intended.

Double failure...a missed opportunity for him, and a stark reminder for me, that I must not abdicate my responsibility to think for myself, even if only for momentary convenience or conflict avoidance. I need to make time to talk with dad about this - just he and I.

During our time together over that weekend in June, we indeed had many hours to talk, during which God gave me an opportunity to share during the majority of our discussion time, my belief in Christ, and how I, dad's first born son, made a decision under the guidance of the Holy Spirit to become a Christian. God even gave us car troubles which forced us into having an extra day during the ride home to address this issue!

> All things work together for good for those who love God, to them who are called according to his purpose (Romans 8:28).

By the end of the weekend, I was exhausted, physically, intellectually, emotionally, and spiritually. Exhausted in-part because of the long drive, hard work, and intense conversation, piled atop the frustration of having car trouble…all expected. I was also fatigued however, due to the sometimes intense debate which dad and I had as I attempted to communicate with him on the content and meaning of the scriptures.

I had my Bible with me, and showed him each of the references that I was drawing his attention to. With practically each reference, however, dad began to argue with me regarding the meaning of the scripture in light of what he had been taught or had come to believe. Through this, there were instances when I was able to constructively address his perceptions and misconceptions. There were others when my patience and grace were not as demonstrable as I would have liked, and where I found myself literally yelling at him as he posed weakly constructed opposition or objections to the scriptures that we were reviewing. While this kind of confrontation was certainly anticipated, and highly likely, given his 40 year adamancy over the folly of Christianity, somehow when it was over, I felt like a bully.

Following that weekend, and in reflection, I asked myself why I felt that way. Certainly, the experience was successful on a number of levels; 1) my father now knows the depth and rationale for my beliefs and that of my wife and children, an understanding which I believe he deserves to have, 2) he was able, if not forced to see actual Biblical scriptures which contradict some of the misconceptions which he has developed or been taught over the years, and 3) I was able to articulate my understandings and beliefs to a critical and somewhat unsympathetic audience of significance.

Despite my consciousness of the success of the experience, and I am quite thankful for God having provided the opportunity, it also forced me to query myself on the anger that I felt during the discussions. As I explored my feelings about this, I realized that my anger was due, in part, to the many apparent impacts which have resulted from his decision to leave Christianity, much of which was based on misconceptions and/or misguided teachings about Christ. Significant impacts which I recognized as sources of frustration for me were of separation and isolation.

I was angry first, because dad made a decision that separated him from a close relationship with God; something that I know is important to him. Aside from the apparent separation from God, there was also separation and conflict, albeit subtle at times, which I recall between my parents and many of us who are family and friends. The decision to leave Christianity has affected, not one, but a minimum of four, and possibly five generations of people (so far) who knowingly, or subconsciously have been influenced. Impacted generations include:

- Mom and dad's relationships with their parents, aunts and uncles who had to adjust to, and accept their decisions. As a child, I witnessed significant conflict on this front, played out on both sides of the family,
- Mom and dad's relationships with their brothers and sisters,
- Myself and each of my 3 siblings in our relationships with our parents, with each other, and our spouses or significant others, and
- Each of our children, who at this point are following our example for whom the religious differences between their grandparents, uncle, aunts and cousins are strained due to differences in beliefs, practices and understandings.

This isolation and separation exists in each of these relationships, though we all proclaim to be committed to having a proper relationship with God. With these differences, there exists a limit to which we can truly and openly communicate, trust, and even pray with one another. So, while on the surface all appears well, it is not.

HEALING PARALYSIS

For what is a man profited, if he shall gain the whole world, and lose his own soul? Or what shall a man give in exchange for his soul? (Matthew 16:26).

Beyond the separation and isolation, I think that I was also angry because of the lack of acceptance and guilt which I know that my wife has felt over the approximate 2 decades of our marriage, as in her mind, she struggles, even now, with feelings that perhaps my parents believe that she somehow abducted their son away from them, luring him off to a religion which they had long ago concluded was a farce, replete with polytheism, worship of a man, and weak-mindedness. Andrea and I have had countless arguments during which she would proclaim that "your parents haven't accepted me" despite my insistence that she was wrong. Both mom and dad love Andrea as their own daughter, have expressed that sentiment to her and to me together and separately, however her sensitivities are real, and certainly real to her. And maybe on some level she is right.

As recently as approximately one year before the North Carolina experience outlined above, (and after 20 years into my marriage) mom said to me in private, "I still think you made a mistake by going into Christianity, and you say that you made the decision yourself, but I believe that you were being pulled. If you actually read the Bible from cover to cover, you would not independently reach the conclusion that Jesus is God." Actually, despite mom's assertion, I had in-fact read the Bible on my own, cover to cover. My first full cover-to-cover reading, completed approximately 10 years earlier, took me two years of independent study, and in so-doing, I reached exactly the conclusion that mom claimed that I would not.

I was also angry because, despite my adult decision to become a Christian, my childhood programming remains an important part of the behavior patterns which I continue to manifest as an adult, and while I recognize that there are positive as well as negative aspects of that programming, much was built on misconceptions, faulty beliefs and teachings about Christ.

So on that day, I felt a sense of outrage as dad made his lack of understanding so abundantly clear. I was not angry simply because of the isolation and separation, not just because of the relationship challenges, and certainly not because of the experiences of my childhood. These are all part of life, and I could have been dealt a far worse hand. I was angry because all of the above was built, not on truth, but on misperceptions, misinformation, and misunderstandings about who Christ was. Dad's decisions, as I understood them that weekend in June, were primarily driven, not by truth and wisdom, but rather by lack of knowledge and understanding! My rational sensibilities, my intellect and ability to think and reason – a part of me which I attribute in-part to the training encouraged by and received from my parents, had been violated. *This made me angry!*

So it was right to have the conversation. But it was wrong for me to allow my anger to present itself during the expected conflict. I was a bully, because while on the surface, one might see two adults (42 and 61 years of age) debating an issue of spiritual significance, the truth was quite different. In reality it was a 42 year old doctorate level university professor, berating a 20 year old high school graduate's life decisions made at a time of confusion, social upheaval and fear. In the nine years served as a professor teaching undergraduate and graduate students, I never treated a student with the level of disrespect that I did my father during that weekend, no matter how serious the infraction. Yet, despite my failure during this interaction, my dad never attempted to pull rank, nor even mention my impudence. *I can and must do better.*

Based upon this, and knowing that I can never again allow the message to be tarnished by the emotions that I was experiencing, I decided to develop a written outline of the scriptures in preparation for a similar discussion with my mother, which occurred approximately 6 months later. I prepared the outline as a means to provide her with a written road map, useful for her own study, thus eliminating her need to rely on memory. I also thought that the written outline would be an excellent way of minimizing her and I as the focal points of the discussion.

Using that outline, and my copies of the Bible, mom and I were able to cover the same material with better communication and without argument, in approximately 3 hours instead of under conflict over 30 hours that it took with dad. Over the three months following that meeting, mom began to listen to audio cassette tapes of the King James Version of the Bible in her car daily to increase her knowledge with the backdrop of the scriptures contained in the prepared outline. Three months after our meeting and after several additional discussions that she initiated with me aimed at improving her understanding of what she was learning, she attended Resurrection Day Service at our church and under the guidance of the Holy Spirit, accepted Christ as her Lord and Savior!

That outline prepared for mom, an outgrowth from my reflections from my meeting with dad, forms the backbone of this book.

***

Foundations

I love my father dearly and have a great deal of respect for he and my mother, who immediately out of high school married as teenagers, and began to raise a family in the turbulence of the 1960's when battles over civil rights, respect for women, and demands for equality for black men was peaking in this country. I can recall vividly being restricted to my home and backyard in East Orange, NJ as uniformed armed soldiers attempted to maintain civil order following the assassination of Dr. Martin Luther King Jr.

I am the oldest child of 4, raised in a home where high levels of self-respect, fear of God, and respect for elders was combined with the unshakable philosophy that "you can have anything as long as you are willing to work for it." My dad owned his own carpentry business, and he required that I regularly help him at worksites from the time that I was about 8 until I left home for college. Dad, even to this day, is one of the strongest men that I know. In extraordinary physical shape, despite 4 decades as a diabetic, he is honest, hardworking and selfless in his support of others. As a boy, I could see these characteristics in him, and his reputation as an honest, clean hard worker served our family well. Dad and mom never smoked, consumed alcohol, nor used illicit drugs, and raised their children to reflect those values. Through all of this, I was able to witness first hand, the value of sacrificing temporary pleasures and enjoyment for long term rewards.

Dad is a man who loved and still loves his family with all of his being; and was always committed to providing his children with as much time and attention as he could, not with quiet time, but rather with highly intense physical activities, always containing life lessons and experiences designed to ensure that we would become capable adults. By age 8, I could ride a motorcycle, ski, roller and ice skate, bowl, and accurately shoot using a bow and arrow and rifle. By the time I was twelve, dad had taught me to drive a standard shift truck, and trusted me to do so in his presence or without. He had also taught me and my siblings to lay vinyl floor tiles, install ceiling tiles, roof shingles and storm windows, and clean-up abandoned homes or parcels of land without supervision. I had participated in sacrificing and preparing lambs for consumption by members of the mosque, and of course, I would be expected to lead the family in prayer in his absence. We all fully participated in fasting during daylight hours during the month of Ramadan annually without fail, even as young children. Through it all, I knew that my dad loved me, though I have no memory of ever hearing him say the words.

As part of these experiences mom and dad programmed me to understand the importance of being responsible for the safety and well-being of those under my care. In many of the above work and recreational activities, there existed a very real potential for life threatening injuries to myself or others if I was not conscious about doing things right. "Safety First" was always taught, and I often wonder if that did not somehow foreshadow my career as a successful safety and health consultant. Accidents do not just happen. An error was made; an error in decision-making or judgment, an error in understanding, communication, or documentation, or a failure to properly prepare, plan or inspect. For her part, mom always reminded me, that I needed to be smarter, harder working, better behaved, more polite, better prepared, and more professional than others, simply to be treated with the same regard. She also impressed upon me, the importance of getting my education, as "they will never be able to take that from you." No excuses!

As the first born, I also experienced, the disciplinary approaches of a young and inexperienced father who was committed to ensuring that this black boy would never grow up to be lazy, nor a thief, substance abuser, or womanizer. In the 60's and 70's his approach may have been characterized as tough discipline. By today's standards, that disciplinary approach would likely be characterized as child abuse, and was probably responsible, in-part, for the ultimate separation and divorce of my parents. During the disciplinary proceedings, dad customarily declared that "you can play the game if you're willing to pay the price" - the intended message; if you don't like the punishment, don't commit the crime.

Survival strategies developed.
- <u>Strategy #1 - Learn to Listen</u>. Quickly discern what is and what is not being said. I learned to read mood, countenance, deportment, and vocal inflection, and to anticipate not just the next question, but also the unstated need of the inquisitor. If I can anticipate that need and quickly begin to move in the direction meeting that need, I will be more successful.
- <u>Strategy #2 - Show that I am Listening</u>. Communicate via verbal and nonverbal cues that the concerns of the person speaking is of importance to me in real-time as the communication is occurring.
- <u>Strategy #3 - Develop Self Discipline and Self Control</u>. If I can make a decision to meet the needs of others quickly, take measured steps toward meeting those needs, and ultimately meet the needs, not merely to the level of their expectation, but rather to the standards of excellence that I have established for myself, while maintaining the momentum to complete the project long after the emotion associated with the initial decision has dissipated, and all while controlling my desires and appetites in accordance with God's will, I will be successful. For me, this was and still is, the pathway from *Liberty* to *Freedom*. Through this, no one external to myself will ever be able to maintain long-term control over my freedom to develop into the person that God intends.
- <u>Strategy #4 – Admit Mistakes Quickly</u>. Inquire as to how I can remedy the situation, and quickly over-deliver.

I was not a perfect child. I did things that even today I regret, but I also knew that the severity of the disciplinary measures often exceeded the level of the infraction. Despite this, I also knew, even then, that my dad was doing his best to raise and protect me. I never once doubted his love for me, and the first chance that I could (the summer that I left home for college), I made the decision to forgive him for the disciplinary excesses, and committed myself to building a great relationship with him based upon love and *mutual* respect. At the same time, I committed that I would always do my very best to be an integral part of my children's lives, that I would be present and involved in their upbringing, much like my parents did for me, but also that my children would never have to endure the harsh physical discipline that often came as part of the package. I did not try to forget about the pain, nor pretend that it didn't happen. I did not repress it. I simply forgave. With that done, I then focused on developing myself into the person that he and others could respect.

During that first summer in college, I quickly realized that there was something very different between myself, and many of my peers (black, white, or otherwise). That something was this:

I had a great advantage over the others because I had a close relationship with my father!

Even now, well into my forties, I still recognize the value of this gift, and see numerous manifestations of it almost daily as I interact with others, despite the realities of my own as well as dad's imperfections.

Today dad and I play golf and take motorcycle rides together, and for his last birthday, I purchased a Honda GoldWing motorcycle that he had been eyeing. He is a super grandfather, and has indicated on a few occasions, regrets for some of the harsh disciplinary modalities. As he has matured, he has grown in many excellent ways. But there is one area where he has not grown. In some ways, the choices that he and mom made as adolescents are still driving the adult man, and significantly paralyzing him from achieving the closeness and richness of his relationship with his heavenly Father.

***

In the opening passage of this book, excerpted from the gospel of Luke, there was a palsy stricken man who could not bring himself to God.

HEALING PARALYSIS

In his case, the paralysis was physical. Dorland's Illustrated Medical Dictionary describes palsy as "paralysis…a persisting qualitative motor disorder…loss or impairment of motor or sensory function due to lesion of the neural or muscular mechanism." Whether due to a congenital, acquired, or traumatic origin, many with paralysis live in a state where the intentions produced by the brain can not be implemented because of an interruption of the signal somewhere between the brain, neural pathway and muscle tissue. Many who recognize themselves in this condition acknowledge the need for support systems (loving family, supportive medical care etc.), and accept that care so that a quality of life can be maximized given the realities of the limitations of the condition. Those in this condition, but who are not aware, may experience difficulties moving in a desired direction or even in sensing a need to move in response to stimuli. Chronic frustration, anxiety or stress due to an inability to meet self or externally-generated expectations on the part of the one who is unknowingly suffering as well as for those with whom that person interacts, may result.

For the man described in the opening, there was more than simply his own physical limitations that presented challenges in getting before Jesus to be healed. There were also the sensory or motor interruptions associated with the crowded conditions of the multitudes of persons; some seeking healing, some spectators, critics and skeptics, political and religious leaders and scholars who were in the pathway preventing the man from getting close enough to Jesus. These conditions were equally important impediments which those persons close to him (friends, family), through their faith, ingenuity and diligence needed to overcome or transcend in order that he may receive the gift from God that he so desperately needed.

Dad is an orthodox Muslim; an evolution from he and my mom's decision to leave the Catholic Church shortly after I was born in the early 1960's (while in their late teenage years) and go into Islam. In my discussions with them regarding the rationale for their decisions, they each cited the Catholic Church's unwillingness (or inability) to explain or clarify the "mystery of the Trinity" coupled with the appeal of the social goals of the civil rights movement and emphasis on black pride and self reliance, as chief among the drivers of their decision to enter Islam. I also sense that the high value placed on caring for one's family which they received from their orientation to the Islamic faith; a sharp contrast to their impressions of popular culture among blacks at that time, also served as a source of motivation for him and mom.

According to dad, the enduring appeal of Islam is its simplicity.

"There is only one God and his name is Allah...God neither begets, nor is he begotten. To worship Christ is to worship a man...the complexities of Christ as the son of God or as a prophet wrongly being worshipped as God himself don't make sense, and obviously contradict each other...and so the Bible contradicts itself. If Jesus was God, then why didn't he just plainly come out and say it! Why would I worship the creation (the Son) instead of the Creator (God Himself), and even worse; the idea of worshiping 3 gods (Holy Ghost?...Trinity?)...And how could eating swine be disallowed in the beginning and then suddenly allowed later? God doesn't change his mind. You Christians are a confused lot, and have got it all wrong!"

By this logic, dad is sure that he has all that he should in his relationship with God, and by doing good works (more than bad works) and obeying God's commandments, the angels assigned to record his deeds will prepare his books for the Day of Judgment, and he will have earned his way into Heaven through being obedient to God's instructions.

As you can likely deduce, I can appreciate the reality of my dad's confusion, and even his 1960's need to find a solution to the pressures of the day so that he could raise a strong family under a defensible set of beliefs. And while I consider the rationale for their leaving Christianity for Islam (confusion, frustration and the appeal of self reliance and black pride) as being critically flawed and indicative of an immature decision making process common among adolescents, and because I know that I am not strong enough to rely upon myself for anything, yet all things are possible through Christ (Philippians 4:13), I can also understand and empathize with their desire to do what they thought was best at the time, given the situation and environment in which they found themselves, and pressures that they were under.

HEALING PARALYSIS

Besides, Jesus himself said

Anyone who heareth the word of the kingdom, and understandeth it not, then cometh the wicked one, and catcheth away that which was sown in his heart (Matthew 13:19).

Consistent with the above, it can be said, that the paralyzed man described in the opening passage may have had two great advantages over my dad; that is, 1) he knew that he needed help, and 2) he knew that he could not get there on his own, but instead needed to trust those close to him, to bring him into the presence of the Lord. My dad, perhaps like so many others who know and believe, without a doubt, that God exists, but have been drawn away or separated by confusion, social issues or fear, may not recognize the degree to which they are separated and live in as great a condition of need as the paralyzed man being lowered through the roof. While the intention is to be obedient to God, they may not have knowledge that there is an interruption or lesion between that mental or spiritually desired intention and the ability to move toward God. And for lack of knowledge they may continue on, bearing burdens that they should not, and indeed can not, bear, all the while not trusting those that know God…all of this, under an illusion of obedience, wisdom and truth.

***

Based upon the above, the scriptures contained in the chapters that follow use the Bible to test the validity of dad's 7 points of opposition to the acceptance of Christ described on the previous page. Specifically, does the Bible actually reveal that Christ is the Son of God? Is the worship of Christ only worship of a man? If Jesus was really the earthly manifestation of God, then why didn't He openly declare it? When we pray in Jesus' name, are we praying to the Creator himself or merely the creation? Why do Christian's reference the Father, Son and Holy Ghost, and is this "Trinity" Biblically justified? Does the Bible contradict itself with regard to who Jesus is? Finally, was the consumption of swine originally disallowed by God, and is it Biblically wrong for Christians to consume this forbidden meat today? The purpose in sharing the selected passages in the chapters that follow, is not to "make him or anyone believe" but rather simply to show where the Bible reveals the Deity of Jesus the Christ. However it is not my will, nor my calling him to Christ, but rather the will of our Father in Heaven to call sons to be heirs of the Kingdom. God through the Holy Spirit, in His own way and in His own time, perhaps unique for each of us, calls only whom He will to come to believe. In this knowledge, I can have peace.

> *No man can come to me, expect the Father which hath sent me draw him: and I will raise him up at the last day* (John 6:44).

Another reason that I believe that it is impossible for me to make him or anyone else a believer, emanates from my formal masters and doctorate level training in industrial hygiene and public health, and my experience as a professor of those disciplines. As a professor, I taught undergraduate and graduate students that adoption of healthy behaviors emanate, in part, from the Health Beliefs of the person (and I consider a building a solid relationship with God to be a healthy behavior, as there can be no more important health indicator than everlasting life).

Health Beliefs: A Precursor to Healthy Decisions and Behaviors

A theoretical model of health behaviors was conceptualized in the 1950's aimed at identifying the resources needed for citizens to better utilize health services, and later to encourage people to assume more healthy lifestyles. This model is termed the "Health Belief Model." Under the Health Belief Model, people will only adopt and maintain healthy behaviors if they:

1. feel that a negative health condition is a realistic possibility for them, and yet can be avoided,
2. have a positive expectation that by taking a recommended action, he/she will avoid a negative health condition, and
3. believe that he/she has the ability and resources to successfully implement the recommended health action.

While this model has been since modified to account for issues of perceived risks and benefits, and self efficacy toward improving or attenuating a person's likelihood of attempting a health behavior, and even further improved to include consideration of Predisposing, Reinforcing and Enabling Factors which lead to effective design of health promotion educational programs, the model in its simplest form, highlights my intellectual and life-learned beliefs as it relates to the acceptance of Christ.

In this context, a Muslim will adopt a more healthy lifestyle (accept Christ) if;
1. the feeling that a significant negative health condition (eternal hell fire) is a realistic possibility for them, and can be avoided,
2. they have adequate knowledge and an expectation that by taking a recommended action (accepting Christ) they can avoid the hell fire, and
3. they believe that they have the capacity and resources necessary to take the action.

Based upon the above, and in light of my own experience, I consider it practically futile for a Christian to approach a Muslim and say "Just Believe that Christ is Lord" as many Christians do and indeed as was often suggested to me. To make such an important health decision based upon that advice only, may be tantamount in the mind of the Muslim, to deciding to "Stop worshiping God, start worshipping a man, and go straight to hell."

Indeed for me, and as an illustration of the application of the Health Belief Model described above, in order to accept Christ, I had to first, <u>recognize the impossibility of pleasing God solely through my actions</u> which included prayer, fasting and numerous other rituals. I realized this first when I was approximately 12 years old.

> One morning, after prayer and in preparation for a day of fasting during the month of Ramadan, I recall crying to God saying "how unfair I feel it is that because of Adam's sin, we all must sin and face the constant threat of hell either by inaction such as failing to perform a required deed (like fasting or prayer), or by actually committing a sinful act. If I could, I would trade places with You, and let you experience the pain and temptation of this world for yourself, and when you failed, I would forgive you."

Next I had to <u>understand that there was a more attainable (and logical)</u>

<u>way to avoid the hellfire</u>, but the understanding of that mechanism took many years (over a decade) to obtain. The protracted length of time for me to gain that understanding was partially a result of my training to distrust practicing Christians, many of whom I believed could not even understand the reference point of the questions that I needed answers to, much less direct me to the answers, coupled with a natural resistance to relying on the advice of others when such a matter of great gravity (salvation of one's soul) depends. Another source of the delay was simply that I needed time to read the Bible, absorb the information, and learn and accept it. Worse, a significant part of the delay was my own shame or embarrassment, stemming from my insecurities, fearing that Christians would "look down" at me if they knew that I was not fully "like them." This non-productive fear prevented me from openly seeking focused guidance earlier.

What I did not understand at the time of my twelve year old plea, but indeed have come to understand over the three decades that followed, is that God had already done what I had asked, and more.

> *God* humbled himself by taking the *form of a human* to live among and teach us, to *manifest his name* on earth, but more importantly, *to experience* the fear, temptation, anguish, and pain, that humans do, and through that human form, made *the ultimate sacrifice*...the ultimate sin offering for His people. That *perfect sin offering* was more perfect than the burnt offerings at the altar, more perfect than the priest's sacrifice on behalf of the congregation, and more perfect than the abstaining from unclean meats of the Old Testament. God's *sacrifice* for our sins was *Himself*, and by allowing us to put His perfect, sinless human form to death, and in death descend into hell *to bear the iniquities* for those whom He has called, He would *pay a ransom*. That ransom, combined with God's perfect love for us, and a healthy dose of *empathy* that comes with God having subjected himself fully to what it means to be human, resulted in a *just mechanism* for the *forgiveness of the sins* which those of us whom He has called to be sons of the kingdom, and through that justification we would have *eternal life*...that eternal life which *God intended* for Adam and Eve from the beginning; from the *foundation of the world*.

Finally, after understanding and then accepting that I could not earn my way to heaven, but that there was in-fact a realistic way to get there, I eventually, through a supportive group including my wife and respected men of the Church, learned that <u>I had the capacity</u> to accomplish salvation. *I only needed to say yes to Christ and accept Him as my Lord and Savior!* Nothing that I had done in the past…and indeed nothing that I had failed to do in the past, would or could prevent or disqualify me from receiving this gift of salvation.

With the increased understanding of who Jesus was, and with assistance of pastors, brothers in Christ, and my wife, I made the decision to accept Christ and committed to publicly acknowledging that decision before my first child was born. By doing this, my wife and I would be able to raise our children with a clear defensible set of beliefs, and not in a state of limbo, paralyzed between two conflicting religious beliefs, leaving them to figure it out for themselves or attempt to blend multiple beliefs together, or to abandon God altogether out of confusion.

✳✳✳

The purpose of this book is not to disparage Islam, Judaism, the Catholic Church or any religion in any way. Rather the purpose is to simply provide a simple focused description of how interested people can begin to learn and understand who Christ really is. This may be of benefit to Christians, Jews, Muslims, Jehovah's Witnesses, agnostics, atheists or others to whom the Lord is calling but who may be paralyzed by past decisions, a life that has been built around prior rituals or disciplines, or who may fear that to accept Christ is to worship a false God or many gods.

The contents of this book are therefore related to only a few issues; not what I think, but rather what the Bible has to say about the following:

- Who is Christ?
- For what Limited Purpose Did he Come to Fulfill during his Brief Time on Earth?
- If Jews and Muslims don't eat Pork, then where in the Bible does it describe that Christian's are allowed this?

Again, the purpose of this book is not to persuade, but rather to assist in increasing *understanding*, for as Jesus said to the Pharisees when they attempted to ensnare him by asking which was the greatest of the commandments, Jesus' reply was:

Thou shalt love the Lord thy God with all thy heart, and with all thy soul, and with all thy mind (Matthew 23:37).

I will only provide a minimum road map, so that the reader can better use their *mind* to better understand who the Bible says that Jesus is, and thus more readily advance along the pathway toward forming a closer relationship with God, and navigate through the morass of skeptics who deny Christ as God himself, manifested on earth and sacrificed to bear the iniquity of the world, perhaps eliminating months, years, or decades from a life in paralysis.

Who Should Consider This Book

This book is obviously intended for anyone seeking to gain a better understanding of who Christ is, including those Muslims, Jews or Jehovah's Witnesses who may believe that Christ was just a prophet, or that He did not die on the cross.

Pastors may find this book particularly helpful when speaking to prospective members of the body of Christ such as those above, whom without question, know and believe that God exists, but may need the specifics of "Is Christ Really God?" Focusing on Christ's teachings on how to, for example, "love your enemy as your brother" though extremely important, may be missing the mark that represents the critical need that these people are desperately searching for. To be sure, teachings such as the above are essential for Christians as we seek to be more like God, but may not get at the critical need for someone who already knows that God exists and that God is good. Churches may also find this book a solid supplement to their Bible study or Baptism classes.

This book is also intended for children or young adults who are

Christians, who may be in high school or college, and who may soon be facing challenges from fellow students, teachers, colleagues, professors, and employers who do not know Christ or may claim that "nowhere in the Bible does it say that Christ is God" or that "you are weak if you worship a white man's God" or other similar rhetoric. Our children and young adults should have easy access to a range of biblical citations that prevent them from falling into these traps. This is true of new believers and for "Christians Since Birth" that may have never had the need to immerse themselves in the question of "who really is Jesus" as they properly followed their parent's decisions on faith. Each child, adolescent and adult should be equipped to defend their faith. The contents of the chapters that follow should be helpful for children and adolescents toward this.

Similarly, spouses or significant others of adults who are seeking to make decisions as to whether or not to accept Christ, may find this book helpful toward understanding some of the challenges or difficulties which that person who is searching may be experiencing, and how they can gently assist without placing themselves in the crosshairs.

I have formatted this book into 7 major sections, organized by topic and presented in sequential order as the verses appear in the Old and New Testaments of the Holy Bible - King James Version. By organizing them in this way, I hope that the reader can begin to see the logical progression from

- Man's closeness with God, to
- Man's separation from God, to
- God's plan and prophecy of redemption through the birth of the Christ, to
- The world's incorrect characterization of Christ as a mere prophet, to
- Christ's proclaiming that He and the Father are one, to
- Christ's sacrifice and resurrection to reconcile Adam's transgression for all who come to believe.
- The teachings of the Apostle Paul regarding Christ, and
- Christ's Cleansing of Un-Clean Meats

The reader should understand that the scriptures presented are not the only Biblical scriptures which address these issues, and indeed do not represent even a majority of such scriptures which appear within the Bible. Instead, they represent exactly the opposite; that is, a small fraction of what the Bible says about these issues, but this fraction speaks directly to me as a man who previously was a Muslim, who needed to have the kind of clarity that is being sought by readers of this book, regarding who Jesus is.

Also understand that I am not addressing the teachings of Jesus for a proper life, nor the Laws of the God's Kingdom (system of management by which God governs and controls everything that He has made; A.E. Fenton), which was the centerpiece of Jesus' teaching when on earth, or even how to pray. Learning to live a life based upon the principles that Jesus modeled for us while on earth, is part of the lifelong struggle that Christians bear. This is advanced Christianity, indeed the *hard* part about being a Christian, and not the subject of this text.

It is suggested that this book be read twice:

1st Reading – Read the *Italicized Discussion Points* provided for each section, followed by the indented **bolded** Bible verses <u>only</u>. By doing this the reader will be able to quickly access; without distraction, specific biblical scriptures addressing the concept being illustrated.

2nd Reading – Re-read the *Italicized Discussion Points* and then read the entire chapter of the Bible in which the bolded indented verses appear to gain perspective on the context of the concept being illustrated. Check the cross references described in the *Italicized Discussion Points* to those in other Chapters indicated, to assist in understanding continuity between Old Testament and New Testament scriptures. Write any thoughts, insights or comments in the "notes" pages which follow each Bible chapter.

After having conducted the above, it is suggested that you use this book, your handwritten notes, and a *Red Letter* copy of the Bible to engage a qualified Pastor in discussion regarding questions that you may have regarding who Jesus is, and what it means to accept Him.

Quick Summary of Organization of the Holy Bible

In order to understand the significance of the information that follows, some knowledge of how the Holy Bible is organized may be helpful. Overall, the Bible is organized into two parts; 1) The Old Testament, beginning at *Genesis* and concluding with *Malachi*, and 2) the New Testament, beginning with *Matthew*, and ending with *Revelation*.

The Old Testament begins with God's creation of the world and Adam and Eve, and proceeds through Satan's deception which lead to Adam's sin and man's separation from God. It continues with the life of Joseph, the enslavement and ultimate release of the Isrealites from Egypt, Moses' leadership through the rise of King David and Solomon and numerous prophets who described the coming of the Savior, born of the lineage of David.

The New Testament begins with the birth of John the Baptist and Jesus and the Gospels (Good News) of Matthew, Mark, Luke and John, which chronicle the life, teachings, death and resurrection of Jesus. Following the Gospels, the book of Acts describes the events which immediately followed Jesus' death, the initial work of the disciples in starting the early Church, and Christ's commissioning of Paul, a former tormentor of the early church, as an apostle to bring the good news of Christ to the Gentiles. Following this, there are 14 books written by the Apostle Paul to the early churches clarifying who Christ is and how to live a Godly life (*Romans* to *Hebrews*). The final 8 books of the New Testament which pertain to Christ, godly living, and the end time war between God and Satan were written by disciples of Christ; Peter, James and John.

That said, lets begin...at the beginning.

CHAPTER 2

Our Inheritance of Adam's Sin

Discussion Point 2.1
God Created Adam
Let us create man in our image. The use of the plural form of the first person pronoun (us and our) reflects a "conversation" between more than one part of a single entity. Note that "image" is not plural, for if it were, one might conclude that there is more than one entity. Not so... There is only one God. (Gen 1:26-28).

***

Genesis Chapter 1

1 In the beginning God created the heaven and the earth. 2 And the earth was without form, and void; and darkness was upon the face of the deep. And the Spirit of God moved upon the face of the waters.

3 And God said, Let there be light: and there was light. 4 And God saw the light, that it was good: and God divided the light from the darkness. 5 And God called the light Day, and the darkness he called Night. And the evening and the morning were the first day.

6 And God said, Let there be a firmament in the midst of the waters, and let it divide the waters from the waters. 7 And God made the firmament, and divided the waters which were under the firmament from the waters which were above the firmament: and it was so. 8 And God called the firmament Heaven. And the evening and the morning were the second day.

9 And God said, Let the waters under the heaven be gathered together unto one place, and let the dry land appear: and it was so. 10 And God called the dry land Earth; and the gathering together of the waters called he Seas: and God saw that it was good. 11 And God said, Let the earth bring forth grass, the herb yielding seed, and the fruit tree yielding fruit after his kind, whose seed is in itself, upon the earth: and it was so. 12 And the earth brought forth grass, and herb yielding seed after his kind, and

the tree yielding fruit, whose seed was in itself, after his kind: and God saw that it was good. *13* And the evening and the morning were the third day.

14 And God said, Let there be lights in the firmament of the heaven to divide the day from the night; and let them be for signs, and for seasons, and for days, and years: *15* And let them be for lights in the firmament of the heaven to give light upon the earth: and it was so. *16* And God made two great lights; the greater light to rule the day, and the lesser light to rule the night: he made the stars also. *17* And God set them in the firmament of the heaven to give light upon the earth, *18* And to rule over the day and over the night, and to divide the light from the darkness: and God saw that it was good. *19* And the evening and the morning were the fourth day.

20 And God said, Let the waters bring forth abundantly the moving creature that hath life, and fowl that may fly above the earth in the open firmament of heaven. *21* And God created great whales, and every living creature that moveth, which the waters brought forth abundantly, after their kind, and every winged fowl after his kind: and God saw that it was good. *22* And God blessed them, saying, Be fruitful, and multiply, and fill the waters in the seas, and let fowl multiply in the earth. *23* And the evening and the morning were the fifth day.

24 And God said, Let the earth bring forth the living creature after his kind, cattle, and creeping thing, and beast of the earth after his kind: and it was so. *25* And God made the beast of the earth after his kind, and cattle after their kind, and every thing that creepeth upon the earth after his kind: and God saw that it was good.

26 And God said, Let us make man in our image, after our likeness: and let them have dominion over the fish of the sea, and over the fowl of the air, and over the cattle, and over all the earth, and over every creeping thing that creepeth upon the earth. 27 So God created man in his own image, in the image of God created he him; male and female created he them. 28 And God blessed them, and God said unto them, Be fruitful, and multiply, and replenish the earth, and subdue it: and have dominion over the fish of the sea, and over the fowl of the air, and over every living thing that moveth upon the earth.

29 And God said, Behold, I have given you every herb bearing seed, which is upon the face of all the earth, and every tree, in the which is the fruit of a tree yielding seed; to you it shall be for meat. *30* And to every beast of the earth, and to every fowl of the air, and to every thing that creepeth upon the earth, wherein there is life, I have given every green herb for meat: and it was so.

31 And God saw every thing that he had made, and, behold, it was very good. And the evening and the morning were the sixth day.

NOTES: GENESIS CHAPTER 1

Discussion Point 2.2
God's Instructions to Adam
Do not eat of the tree of knowledge of good and evil or you will surely die (Gen 2:16-17).

Discussion Point 2.3
God Creates Eve
So that Adam would have a companion and helper (Gen 2:18-25).

***

Genesis Chapter 2

1 Thus the heavens and the earth were finished, and all the host of them. *2* And on the seventh day God ended his work which he had made; and he rested on the seventh day from all his work which he had made. *3* And God blessed the seventh day, and sanctified it: because that in it he had rested from all his work which God created and made. *4* These are the generations of the heavens and of the earth when they were created, in the day that the LORD God made the earth and the heavens, *5* And every plant of the field before it was in the earth, and every herb of the field before it grew: for the LORD God had not caused it to rain upon the earth, and there was not a man to till the ground. *6* But there went up a mist from the earth, and watered the whole face of the ground. *7* And the LORD God formed man of the dust of the ground, and breathed into his nostrils the breath of life; and man became a living soul. *8* And the LORD God planted a garden eastward in Eden; and there he put the man whom he had formed. *9* And out of the ground made the LORD God to grow every tree that is pleasant to the sight, and good for food; the tree of life also in the midst of the garden, and the tree of knowledge of good and evil. *10* And a river went out of Eden to water the garden; and from thence it was parted, and became into four heads. *11* The name of the first is Pison: that is it which compasseth the whole land of Havilah, where there is gold; *12* And the gold of that land is good: there is bdellium and the onyx stone. *13* And the name of the second river is Gihon: the same is it that compasseth the whole land of Ethiopia. *14* And the name of the third river is Hiddekel: that is it which goeth toward the east of Assyria. And the fourth river is Euphrates. *15* And the LORD God took the man, and put him into the garden of Eden to dress it and to keep it.

16 And the LORD God commanded the man, saying, Of every tree of the garden thou mayest freely eat: 17 But of the tree of the knowledge of good and evil, thou shalt not eat of it: for in the day that thou eatest thereof thou shalt surely die. 18 And the LORD God said, It is not good that the man should be alone; I will make him an help meet for him. 19 And out of the ground the LORD God formed every beast of the field, and every fowl of the air; and brought them unto Adam to see what he would call them: and whatsoever Adam called every living creature, that was the name thereof. 20 And Adam gave names to all cattle, and to the fowl of the air, and to every beast of the field; but for Adam there was not found an help meet for him. 21 And the LORD God caused a deep sleep to fall upon Adam, and he slept: and he took one of his ribs, and closed up the flesh instead thereof; 22 And the rib, which the LORD God had taken from man, made he a woman, and brought her unto the man. 23 And Adam said, This is now bone of my bones, and flesh of my flesh: she shall be called Woman, because she was taken out of Man. 24 Therefore shall a man leave his father and his mother, and shall cleave unto his wife: and they shall be one flesh. 25 And they were both naked, the man and his wife, and were not ashamed.

NOTES: GENESIS CHAPTER 2

Discussion Point 2.4
Satan Deceives Adam and Eve
Satan, having taken the form of the serpent, persuades the woman that she will not surely die, but rather that her eyes would be opened and that they would be as gods (Gen 3:1-5).

Discussion Point 2.5
Adam and Eve Become Separated from God.
Eve took and ate the fruit and also convinced Adam to eat of it. When they did this, they knew that they were naked, and in response, hid from God. This represents Adam's first sin and signifies the death of the part of Adam's compound life that was in union with God (Gen 3:6-7).

Discussion Point 2.6
God Condemns Satan
As punishment for Satan beguiling Adam and Eve, God curses the serpent to a life of eating dust, and declares that there will be enmity between the seed of the woman and Satan's seed, and that her seed will bruise Satan's head and that Satan's head will bruise her seed's heal. This is God's first indication of the coming of a Redeemer, born to mankind as an offspring of Eve to ultimately destroy Satan, who has interfered with and inserted himself between man and God (Gen 3:14-15).

Discussion Point 2.7
God Promises a Remedy to Reconcile Man to Eternal Life
After condemning Satan and promising a Redeemer through the offspring of Eve, God then says (to himself, also in plural pronoun form), "now man has become like one of us, to know good and evil" and that because of that knowledge he must reach forth and take of the hold the tree of life, so that he can live forever (Gen 3:22).

✳✳✳

Genesis Chapter 3

1 Now the serpent was more subtil than any beast of the field which the LORD God had made. And he said unto the woman, Yea, hath God said, Ye shall not eat of every tree of the garden? *2* And the woman said unto the serpent, We may eat of the fruit of the trees of the garden: *3* But of the fruit of the tree which is in the midst of the garden, God hath said, Ye shall not eat of it, neither shall ye touch it, lest ye die. *4* And the serpent said unto the woman, Ye shall not surely die: *5* For God doth know that in the day ye eat thereof, then your eyes shall be opened, and ye shall be as gods, knowing good and evil. *6* And when the woman saw that the tree was good for food, and that it was pleasant to the eyes, and a tree to be desired to make one wise, she took of the fruit thereof, and did eat, and gave also unto her husband with her; and he did eat. *7* And the eyes of them both were opened, and they knew that they were naked; and they sewed fig leaves together, and made themselves aprons.

8 And they heard the voice of the LORD God walking in the garden in the cool of the day: and Adam and his wife hid themselves from the presence of the LORD God amongst the trees of the garden. *9* And the LORD God called unto Adam, and said unto him, Where art thou? *10* And he said, I heard thy voice in the garden, and I was afraid, because I was naked; and I hid myself. *11* And he said, Who told thee that thou wast naked? Hast thou eaten of the tree, whereof I commanded thee that thou shouldest not eat? *12* And the man said, The woman whom thou gavest to be with me, she gave me of the tree, and I did eat. *13* And the LORD God said unto the woman, What is this that thou hast done? And the woman said, The serpent beguiled me, and I did eat.

14 And the LORD God said unto the serpent, Because thou hast done this, thou art cursed above all cattle, and above every beast of the field; upon thy belly shalt thou go, and dust shalt thou eat all the days of thy life: *15* **And I will put enmity be-**

tween thee and the woman, and between thy seed and her seed; it shall bruise thy head, and thou shalt bruise his heel.

16 Unto the woman he said, I will greatly multiply thy sorrow and thy conception; in sorrow thou shalt bring forth children; and thy desire shall be to thy husband, and he shall rule over thee. 17 And unto Adam he said, Because thou hast hearkened unto the voice of thy wife, and hast eaten of the tree, of which I commanded thee, saying, Thou shalt not eat of it: cursed is the ground for thy sake; in sorrow shalt thou eat of it all the days of thy life; 18 Thorns also and thistles shall it bring forth to thee; and thou shalt eat the herb of the field; 19 In the sweat of thy face shalt thou eat bread, till thou return unto the ground; for out of it wast thou taken: for dust thou art, and unto dust shalt thou return. 20 And Adam called his wife's name Eve; because she was the mother of all living. 21 Unto Adam also and to his wife did the LORD God make coats of skins, and clothed them.

22 And the LORD God said, Behold, the man is become as one of us, to know good and evil: and now, lest he put forth his hand, and take also of the tree of life, and eat, and live for ever:

23 Therefore the LORD God sent him forth from the garden of Eden, to till the ground from whence he was taken. 24 So he drove out the man; and he placed at the east of the garden of Eden Cherubims, and a flaming sword which turned every way, to keep the way of the tree of life.

NOTES: GENESIS CHAPTER 3

CHAPTER 3

The Prophecy of the Redeemer

From the previous chapter, we saw that God created man and woman in his own likeness, but that Satan inserted himself into the otherwise perfect communion between man and God. When this occurred, Adam committed the original sin which caused man to be separated from God, losing a part of his life, and condemning his seed to hardships caused by being separated.

We also saw in Genesis, that God eternally cursed Satan for this infraction, and proclaimed that Eve's offspring would become Satan's eternal enemy, and would ultimately defeat Satan as his own heel is bruised on Satan's head in so doing. Finally, God, in discussion with himself reveals that because of man's knowledge of good and evil, he (man) must reach forth and accept the tree of life, to have eternal life with God (see Genesis 3:22 and Revelation 22:14).

In this next section, I highlight a few of the Old Testament prophecies of the coming of the Redeemer (Christ). These are but a few of the instances where such prophecies are contained, but stood out for me, as I tried to understand who Jesus is. The prophecies listed in this section are contained in the books of 2nd Samuel (1000 B.C.), I Chronicles (450 B.C.) and Isaiah (700 B.C.).

Discussion Point 3.1
God will Establish His Throne Through David's Seed
God reveals to King David through the Prophet Nathan, that after David's death God will establish through David's seed, His Kingdom which will build a house for God's name and which will be established forever. Here God says that "I will be his father, and he shall be my son" (2 Samuel 7:12-16).

***

2 Samuel Chapter 7

1 And it came to pass, when the king sat in his house, and the LORD had given him rest round about from all his enemies; 2 That the king said unto Nathan the prophet, See now, I dwell in an house of cedar, but the ark of God dwelleth within curtains. 3 And Nathan said to the king, Go, do all that is in thine heart; for the LORD is with thee. 4 And it came to pass that night, that the word of the LORD came unto Nathan, saying, 5 Go and tell my servant David, Thus saith the LORD, Shalt thou build me an house for me to dwell in? 6 Whereas I have not dwelt in any house since the time that I brought up the children of Israel out of Egypt, even to this day, but have walked in a tent and in a tabernacle. 7 In all the places wherein I have walked with all the children of Israel spake I a word with any of the tribes of Israel, whom I commanded to feed my people Israel, saying, Why build ye not me an house of cedar? 8 Now therefore so shalt thou say unto my servant David, Thus saith the LORD of hosts, I took thee from the sheepcote, from following the sheep, to be ruler over my people, over Israel: 9 And I was with thee whithersoever thou wentest, and have cut off all thine enemies out of thy sight, and have made thee a great name, like unto the name of the great men that are in the earth. 10 Moreover I will appoint a place for my people Israel, and will plant them, that they may dwell in a place of their own, and move no more; neither shall the children of wickedness afflict them any more, as beforetime, 11 And as since the time that I commanded judges to be over my people Israel, and have caused thee to rest from all thine enemies. Also the LORD telleth thee that he will make thee an house.

HEALING PARALYSIS

12 And when thy days be fulfilled, and thou shalt sleep with thy fathers, I will set up thy seed after thee, which shall proceed out of thy bowels, and I will establish his kingdom. *13* He shall build an house for my name, and I will stablish the throne of his kingdom for ever. *14* I will be his father, and he shall be my son. If he commit iniquity, I will chasten him with the rod of men, and with the stripes of the children of men: *15* But my mercy shall not depart away from him, as I took it from Saul, whom I put away before thee. *16* And thine house and thy kingdom shall be established for ever before thee: thy throne shall be established for ever.

17 According to all these words, and according to all this vision, so did Nathan speak unto David. *18* Then went king David in, and sat before the LORD, and he said, Who am I, O Lord GOD? and what is my house, that thou hast brought me hitherto? *19* And this was yet a small thing in thy sight, O Lord GOD; but thou hast spoken also of thy servant's house for a great while to come. And is this the manner of man, O Lord GOD? *20* And what can David say more unto thee? for thou, Lord GOD, knowest thy servant. *21* For thy word's sake, and according to thine own heart, hast thou done all these great things, to make thy servant know them. *22* Wherefore thou art great, O LORD God: for there is none like thee, neither is there any God beside thee, according to all that we have heard with our ears. *23* And what one nation in the earth is like thy people, even like Israel, whom God went to redeem for a people to himself, and to make him a name, and to do for you great things and terrible, for thy land, before thy people, which thou redeemedst to thee from Egypt, from the nations and their gods? *24* For thou hast confirmed to thyself thy people Israel to be a people unto thee for ever: and thou, LORD, art become their God. *25* And now, O LORD God, the word that thou hast spoken concerning thy servant, and concerning his house, establish it for ever, and do as thou hast said. *26* And let thy name be magnified for ever, saying, The LORD of hosts is the God over Israel: and let the house of thy servant David be established before thee. *27* For thou, O LORD of hosts, God of Israel, hast revealed to thy servant, saying, I will build thee an house: therefore hath thy servant found in his heart to pray this prayer unto thee.

28 And now, O Lord GOD, thou art that God, and thy words be true, and thou hast promised this goodness unto thy servant: 29 Therefore now let it please thee to bless the house of thy servant, that it may continue for ever before thee: for thou, O Lord GOD, hast spoken it: and with thy blessing let the house of thy servant be blessed for ever.

NOTES: 2 SAMUEL CHAPTER 7

Discussion Point 3.2
David Conveys Gods Prophecy
David describes to Solomon his instructions for Solomon to build the temple and that through his seed, God will establish the throne of his kingdom forever (1 Chronicles 22:10).

***

<u>1 Chronicles Chapter 22</u>

*1*Then David said, This is the house of the LORD God, and this is the altar of the burnt offering for Israel. 2 And David commanded to gather together the strangers that were in the land of Israel; and he set masons to hew wrought stones to build the house of God. 3 And David prepared iron in abundance for the nails for the doors of the gates, and for the joinings; and brass in abundance without weight; *4* Also cedar trees in abundance: for the Zidonians and they of Tyre brought much cedar wood to David. *5* And David said, Solomon my son is young and tender, and the house that is to be builded for the LORD must be exceeding magnifical, of fame and of glory throughout all countries: I will therefore now make preparation for it. So David prepared abundantly before his death. 6 Then he called for Solomon his son, and charged him to build an house for the LORD God of Israel. 7 And David said to Solomon, My son, as for me, it was in my mind to build an house unto the name of the LORD my God: *8* But the word of the LORD came to me, saying, Thou hast shed blood abundantly, and hast made great wars: thou shalt not build an house unto my name, because thou hast shed much blood upon the earth in my sight. *9* Behold, a son shall be born to thee, who shall be a man of rest; and I will give him rest from all his enemies round about: for his name shall be Solomon, and I will give peace and quietness unto Israel in his days.

10 He shall build an house for my name; and he shall be my son, and I will be his father; and I will establish the throne of his kingdom over Israel for ever.

11 Now, my son, the LORD be with thee; and prosper thou, and build the house of the LORD thy God, as he hath said of thee. *12* Only the LORD give thee wisdom and understanding, and give thee charge concerning Israel, that thou mayest keep the law of the LORD thy God. *13* Then shalt thou prosper, if thou takest heed to fulfil the statutes and judgments which the LORD charged Moses with concerning Israel: be strong, and of good courage; dread not, nor be dismayed. *14* Now, behold, in my trouble I have prepared for the house of the LORD an hundred thousand talents of gold, and a thousand thousand talents of silver; and of brass and iron without weight; for it is in abundance: timber also and stone have I prepared; and thou mayest add thereto. *15* Moreover there are workmen with thee in abundance, hewers and workers of stone and timber, and all manner of cunning men for every manner of work. *16* Of the gold, the silver, and the brass, and the iron, there is no number. Arise therefore, and be doing, and the LORD be with thee.

17 David also commanded all the princes of Israel to help Solomon his son, saying, *18* Is not the LORD your God with you? and hath he not given you rest on every side? for he hath given the inhabitants of the land into mine hand; and the land is subdued before the LORD, and before his people. *19* Now set your heart and your soul to seek the LORD your God; arise therefore, and build ye the sanctuary of the LORD God, to bring the ark of the covenant of the LORD, and the holy vessels of God, into the house that is to be built to the name of the LORD.

NOTES: 1 CHRONICLES CHAPTER 22

Discussion Point 3.3
The Redeemer shall be Born of a Virgin
In the book of Isaiah, (approximately 700 years before the birth of Christ) the prophet Isaiah receives from God, a vision concerning the coming of the Redeemer, saying "The Lord himself shall give you a sign; behold a virgin shall conceive, and bear a son and shall call his name Immanuel" (Isaiah 7:13-14).

***

Isaiah Chapter 7

1 And it came to pass in the days of Ahaz the son of Jotham, the son of Uzziah, king of Judah, that Rezin the king of Syria, and Pekah the son of Remaliah, king of Israel, went up toward Jerusalem to war against it, but could not prevail against it. 2 And it was told the house of David, saying, Syria is confederate with Ephraim. And his heart was moved, and the heart of his people, as the trees of the wood are moved with the wind. 3 Then said the LORD unto Isaiah, Go forth now to meet Ahaz, thou, and Shear-jashub thy son, at the end of the conduit of the upper pool in the highway of the fuller's field; 4 And say unto him, Take heed, and be quiet; fear not, neither be fainthearted for the two tails of these smoking firebrands, for the fierce anger of Rezin with Syria, and of the son of Remaliah. 5 Because Syria, Ephraim, and the son of Remaliah, have taken evil counsel against thee, saying, 6 Let us go up against Judah, and vex it, and let us make a breach therein for us, and set a king in the midst of it, even the son of Tabeal: 7 Thus saith the Lord GOD, It shall not stand, neither shall it come to pass. 8 For the head of Syria is Damascus, and the head of Damascus is Rezin; and within threescore and five years shall Ephraim be broken, that it be not a people. 9 And the head of Ephraim is Samaria, and the head of Samaria is Remaliah's son. If ye will not believe, surely ye shall not be established.

10 Moreover the LORD spake again unto Ahaz, saying, 11 Ask thee a sign of the LORD thy God; ask it either in the depth, or in the height above. 12 But Ahaz said, I will not ask, neither will I tempt the LORD.

13 And he said, Hear ye now, O house of David; Is it a small thing for you to weary men, but will ye weary my God also?

***14** Therefore the Lord himself shall give you a sign; Behold, a virgin shall conceive, and bear a son, and shall call his name Immanuel.*

15 Butter and honey shall he eat, that he may know to refuse the evil, and choose the good. 16 For before the child shall know to refuse the evil, and choose the good, the land that thou abhorrest shall be forsaken of both her kings.

17 The LORD shall bring upon thee, and upon thy people, and upon thy father's house, days that have not come, from the day that Ephraim departed from Judah; even the king of Assyria. 18 And it shall come to pass in that day, that the LORD shall hiss for the fly that is in the uttermost part of the rivers of Egypt, and for the bee that is in the land of Assyria. 19 And they shall come, and shall rest all of them in the desolate valleys, and in the holes of the rocks, and upon all thorns, and upon all bushes. 20 In the same day shall the Lord shave with a razor that is hired, namely, by them beyond the river, by the king of Assyria, the head, and the hair of the feet: and it shall also consume the beard. 21 And it shall come to pass in that day, that a man shall nourish a young cow, and two sheep; 22 And it shall come to pass, for the abundance of milk that they shall give he shall eat butter: for butter and honey shall every one eat that is left in the land. 23 And it shall come to pass in that day, that every place shall be, where there were a thousand vines at a thousand silverlings, it shall even be for briers and thorns. 24 With arrows and with bows shall men come thither; because all the land shall become briers and thorns. 25 And on all hills that shall be digged with the mattock, there shall not come thither the fear of briers and thorns: but it shall be for the sending forth of oxen, and for the treading of lesser cattle.

NOTES: ISAIAH CHAPTER 7

Discussion Point 3.4
His name shall be called the Mighty God, Everlasting Father
Further description to the Prophet Isaiah about the coming Christ: For unto us a child is born, unto us a son is given and the government shall be upon his shoulder: and his name shall be called Wonderful, Counselor, the mighty God, The Everlasting Father, The Prince of Peace (Isaiah 9:6-7).

***

<u>Isaiah Chapter 9</u>

1 Nevertheless the dimness shall not be such as was in her vexation, when at the first he lightly afflicted the land of Zebulun and the land of Naphtali, and afterward did more grievously afflict her by the way of the sea, beyond Jordan, in Galilee of the nations. *2* The people that walked in darkness have seen a great light: they that dwell in the land of the shadow of death, upon them hath the light shined. *3* Thou hast multiplied the nation, and not increased the joy: they joy before thee according to the joy in harvest, and as men rejoice when they divide the spoil. *4* For thou hast broken the yoke of his burden, and the staff of his shoulder, the rod of his oppressor, as in the day of Midian. *5* For every battle of the warrior is with confused noise, and garments rolled in blood; but this shall be with burning and fuel of fire.

> **6 For unto us a child is born, unto us a son is given: and the government shall be upon his shoulder: and his name shall be called Wonderful, Counsellor, The mighty God, The everlasting Father, The Prince of Peace. 7 Of the increase of his government and peace there shall be no end, upon the throne of David, and upon his kingdom, to order it, and to establish it with judgment and with justice from henceforth even for ever. The zeal of the LORD of hosts will perform this.**

8 The Lord sent a word into Jacob, and it hath lighted upon Israel. *9* And all the people shall know, even Ephraim and the inhabitant of Samaria, that say in the pride and stoutness of heart, *10* The bricks are fallen down, but we will build with hewn stones: the sycomores are cut down, but we will change them into cedars. *11* Therefore the LORD shall set up the

HEALING PARALYSIS

adversaries of Rezin against him, and join his enemies together; *12* The Syrians before, and the Philistines behind; and they shall devour Israel with open mouth. For all this his anger is not turned away, but his hand is stretched out still. *13* For the people turneth not unto him that smiteth them, neither do they seek the LORD of hosts. *14* Therefore the LORD will cut off from Israel head and tail, branch and rush, in one day. *15* The ancient and honourable, he is the head; and the prophet that teacheth lies, he is the tail. *16* For the leaders of this people cause them to err; and they that are led of them are destroyed. *17* Therefore the Lord shall have no joy in their young men, neither shall have mercy on their fatherless and widows: for every one is an hypocrite and an evildoer, and every mouth speaketh folly. For all this his anger is not turned away, but his hand is stretched out still. *18* For wickedness burneth as the fire: it shall devour the briers and thorns, and shall kindle in the thickets of the forest, and they shall mount up like the lifting up of smoke. *19* Through the wrath of the LORD of hosts is the land darkened, and the people shall be as the fuel of the fire: no man shall spare his brother. *20* And he shall snatch on the right hand, and be hungry; and he shall eat on the left hand, and they shall not be satisfied: they shall eat every man the flesh of his own arm: *21* Manasseh, Ephraim; and Ephraim, Manasseh: and they together shall be against Judah. For all this his anger is not turned away, but his hand is stretched out still.

NOTES: ISAIAH CHAPTER 9

Discussion Point 3.5
He Shall Open Not His Mouth and Shall Bear the Sins for Us All
Prophet Isaiah's detailed description of who Christ is and why He came...(grow up before him having no comliness), and why he came (borne our griefs, wounded for our transgressions,— with his stripes we are healed), and that the Lord has laid on him the iniquity of us all. (Isaiah 53:1-6).
Isaiah goes on to describe why Jesus did not declare his "innocence" to Pontius Pilate or the other accusers: so that we can make his soul an offering for sin. He opened not his mouth...brought as a lamb to the slaughter... Yet it pleased the Lord to bruise him; he hath put him to grief; when thou shalt make his soul an offering for sin. he shall see his seed, he shall prolong his days, and the pleasure of the Lord shall prosper in his hand. (Isaiah 53:7-12)

***

Isaiah Chapter 53

1 Who hath believed our report and to whom is the arm of the LORD revealed? 2 For he shall grow up before him as a tender plant, and as a root out of a dry ground: he hath no form nor comeliness; and when we shall see him, there is no beauty that we should desire him. 3 He is despised and rejected of men; a man of sorrows, and acquainted with grief: and we hid as it were our faces from him; he was despised, and we esteemed him not. 4 Surely he hath borne our griefs, and carried our sorrows: yet we did esteem him stricken, smitten of God, and afflicted. 5 But he was wounded for our transgressions, he was bruised for our iniquities: the chastisement of our peace was upon him; and with his stripes we are healed. 6 All we like sheep have gone astray; we have turned every one to his own way; and the LORD hath laid on him the iniquity of us all.
7 He was oppressed, and he was afflicted, yet he opened not his mouth: he is brought as a lamb to the slaughter, and as a sheep before her shearers is dumb, so he openeth not his mouth. 8 He was taken from prison and from judgment: and who shall declare his generation? for he was cut off out of the land of the living: for the transgression of my people was he stricken. 9 And he made his grave with the wicked, and with

the rich in his death; because he had done no violence, neither was any deceit in his mouth.

10 Yet it pleased the LORD to bruise him; he hath put him to grief: when thou shalt make his soul an offering for sin, he shall see his seed, he shall prolong his days, and the pleasure of the LORD shall prosper in his hand. *11* He shall see of the travail of his soul, and shall be satisfied: by his knowledge shall my righteous servant justify many; for he shall bear their iniquities. *12* Therefore will I divide him a portion with the great, and he shall divide the spoil with the strong; because he hath poured out his soul unto death: and he was numbered with the transgressors; and he bare the sin of many, and made intercession for the transgressors.

NOTES: ISAIAH CHAPTER 53

CHAPTER 4

God's Descent to Earth (in His own words)

From the previous chapter we saw several Old Testament prophecies of the coming of the Christ.

Christ's coming was foretold to David as the seed whose Kingdom would be established for ever, and on whose shoulders the Government would rest. David was instructed that "He shall build an house for my name. I shall be His Father and he shall be my son. His name shall be Wonderful Counselor, the Mighty God, the Everlasting Father."

We also saw that the Christ would be born, without apparent beauty or regard, to bear the iniquity of mankind, and that he would suffer for our transgressions and through his suffering we would receive justification. It was proclaimed that he would not speak in his defense when accused, and would be as the lamb brought to slaughter for the iniquity of mankind. For those who place his soul for an offering for sin, there would be prolonged days and the blessings of the father.

Note the continuity between the Old Testament Prophesies cited in Chapter 3 with God's plan for redemption described in Chapter 2 (Genesis 3:14-22).

In this chapter, we will explore Jesus' own words regarding salvation. In the early chapters of the Gospels (Matthew, Mark, Luke, & John) Jesus teaches as one having knowledge of the Father, then as one who knows the Father, as he explains that those seeking everlasting life through strict adherence to the commandments of Moses are still in sin, and can not, through those actions alone, enter the Kingdom of Heaven. In the later chapters, you will notice that Jesus increasingly speaks as one having authority and not as simply a messenger, and that "I and the Father are One" and that he is the Christ that the Old Testament prophesied and has come to fulfill; a claim which ultimately leads the Jews to decide to put him to death for blasphemy.

Please note that scripture text (not discussion point text) which appears in *italics* indicates the word's of Jesus himself.

Discussion Point 4.1
Jesus Came to Fulfill the Law
Think not that I am come to destroy the Law, or the prophets: I am not come to destroy but to fulfill (Matthew 5:17-18).

Discussion Point 4.2
Literal Compliance with the Law is not Enough
Jesus is telling the disciples that unless their righteousness exceeds that of the Pharisees and scribes that they will not enter the Kingdom of heaven (Matthew 5:19-20).

Discussion Point 4.3
All Have Sinned
Literal compliance with the commandments is not sufficient to enter Heaven, and that even those who believe they are in compliance have sinned (Matthew 5:21-48).

***

Matthew Chapter 5

1 And seeing the multitudes, he went up into a mountain: and when he was set, his disciples came unto him: 2 And he opened his mouth, and taught them, saying, *3 Blessed are the poor in spirit: for theirs is the kingdom of heaven. 4 Blessed are they that mourn: for they shall be comforted. 5 Blessed are the meek: for they shall inherit the earth. 6 Blessed are they which do hunger and thirst after righteousness: for they shall be filled. 7 Blessed are the merciful: for they shall obtain mercy. 8 Blessed are the pure in heart: for they shall see God. 9 Blessed are the peacemakers: for they shall be called the children of God. 10 Blessed are they which are persecuted for righteousness' sake: for theirs is the kingdom of heaven. 11 Blessed are ye, when men shall revile you, and persecute you, and shall say all manner of evil against you falsely, for my sake. 12 Rejoice, and be exceeding glad: for great is your reward in heaven: for so persecuted they the prophets which were before you. 13 Ye are the salt of the earth: but if the salt have lost his savour, wherewith shall it be salted? it is thenceforth good for nothing, but to be cast out, and to be trodden under foot of men. 14 Ye are the light of the world. A city that is set on an hill cannot be hid. 15 Neither do men light a candle, and put it under a bushel, but on a candlestick; and it giveth light unto all that are in the house. 16 Let your light so shine before men, that they may see your good works, and glorify your Father which is in heaven.*

17 Think not that I am come to destroy the law, or the prophets: I am not come to destroy, but to fulfil. 18 For verily I say unto you, Till heaven and earth pass, one jot or one tittle shall in no wise pass from the law, till all be fulfilled. 19 Whosoever therefore shall break one of these least commandments, and shall teach men so, he shall be called the least in the kingdom of heaven: but whosoever shall do and teach them, the same shall be called great in the kingdom of heaven. 20 For I say unto you, That except your righteousness shall exceed the righteousness of the scribes and Pharisees, ye shall in no case enter into the kingdom of heaven.
21 Ye have heard that it was said by them of old time, Thou shalt not kill; and whosoever shall kill shall be in danger of the judgment: 22 But I say unto you, That whosoever is angry with his brother without a cause shall be in danger of the judgment: and whosoever shall say to his brother, Raca, shall be in danger of the council: but whosoever shall say, Thou fool, shall be in danger of hell fire. 23 Therefore if thou bring thy gift to the altar, and there rememberest that thy brother hath ought against thee; 24 Leave there thy gift before the altar, and go thy way; first be reconciled to thy brother, and then come and offer thy gift. 25 Agree with thine adversary quickly, whiles thou art in the way with him; lest at any time the adversary deliver thee to the judge, and the judge deliver thee to the officer, and thou be cast into prison. 26 Verily I say unto thee, Thou shalt by no means come out thence, till thou hast paid the uttermost farthing.
27 Ye have heard that it was said by them of old time, Thou shalt not commit adultery: 28 But I say unto you, That whosoever looketh on a woman to lust after her hath committed adultery with her already in his heart. 29 And if thy right eye offend thee, pluck it out, and cast it from thee: for it is profitable for thee that one of thy members should perish, and not that thy whole body should be cast into hell. 30 And if thy right hand offend thee, cut it off, and cast it from thee: for it is profitable for thee that one of thy members should perish, and not that thy whole body should be cast into hell. 31 It hath been said, Whosoever shall put away his wife, let him give her a writing of divorcement: 32 But I say unto you, That whosoever shall put away his wife, saving for the cause of fornication, causeth her to commit adultery: and whosoever shall marry her that is divorced committeth adultery.
33 Again, ye have heard that it hath been said by them of old time, Thou

shalt not forswear thyself, but shalt perform unto the Lord thine oaths: 34 But I say unto you, Swear not at all; neither by heaven; for it is God's throne: 35 Nor by the earth; for it is his footstool: neither by Jerusalem; for it is the city of the great King. 36 Neither shalt thou swear by thy head, because thou canst not make one hair white or black. 37 But let your communication be, Yea, yea; Nay, nay: for whatsoever is more than these cometh of evil.

38 Ye have heard that it hath been said, An eye for an eye, and a tooth for a tooth: 39 But I say unto you, That ye resist not evil: but whosoever shall smite thee on thy right cheek, turn to him the other also. 40 And if any man will sue thee at the law, and take away thy coat, let him have thy cloke also. 41 And whosoever shall compel thee to go a mile, go with him twain. 42 Give to him that asketh thee, and from him that would borrow of thee turn not thou away.

43 Ye have heard that it hath been said, Thou shalt love thy neighbour, and hate thine enemy. 44 But I say unto you, Love your enemies, bless them that curse you, do good to them that hate you, and pray for them which despitefully use you, and persecute you; 45 That ye may be the children of your Father which is in heaven: for he maketh his sun to rise on the evil and on the good, and sendeth rain on the just and on the unjust. 46 For if ye love them which love you, what reward have ye? do not even the publicans the same? 47 And if ye salute your brethren only, what do ye more than others? do not even the publicans so? 48 Be ye therefore perfect, even as your Father which is in heaven is perfect.

NOTES: MATTHEW CHAPTER 5

Discussion Point 4.4
Jesus begins to speak of himself as God while acknowledging God the Father
Not every one that saith unto me Lord, Lord shall enter into the kingdom of heaven; but he that doeth the will of my Father which is in heaven. Many will say to me in that day, Lord, Lord have we not prophesied in thy name, and in thy name have cast out devils? And in thy name done many wonderful works? And then will I profess unto them, I never knew you: depart from me, ye that work iniquity (Matt 7:21-22).

Discussion Point 4.5
Everyone who hears and conforms to Jesus' instructions will be blessed.
Those who do not shall be likened to a foolish man who builds his house on the sand. (Matt 7:23-27)
Note Jesus' use of I and me (1st person pronouns) indicating that He has the authority for judgment.

✲✲✲

Matthew Chapter 7

1 Judge not, that ye be not judged. 2 For with what judgment ye judge, ye shall be judged: and with what measure ye mete, it shall be measured to you again. 3 And why beholdest thou the mote that is in thy brother's eye, but considerest not the beam that is in thine own eye? 4 Or how wilt thou say to thy brother, Let me pull out the mote out of thine eye; and, behold, a beam is in thine own eye? 5 Thou hypocrite, first cast out the beam out of thine own eye; and then shalt thou see clearly to cast out the mote out of thy brother's eye. 6 Give not that which is holy unto the dogs, neither cast ye your pearls before swine, lest they trample them under their feet, and turn again and rend you. 7 Ask, and it shall be given you; seek, and ye shall find; knock, and it shall be opened unto you: 8 For every one that asketh receiveth; and he that seeketh findeth; and to him that knocketh it shall be opened. 9 Or what man is there of you, whom if his son ask bread, will he give him a stone? 10 Or if he ask a fish, will he give him a serpent? 11 If ye then, being evil, know how to give good gifts unto your children, how much more shall your Father which is in heaven give good things to them that ask him? 12 Therefore all things whatsoever ye would that men should do to you, do ye even so to them: for this is the law and the prophets. 13 Enter ye in at the strait gate: for wide is the gate, and broad is the way, that leadeth to destruction, and many there be which go in thereat: 14 Because strait is the gate, and narrow is the way, which leadeth unto life, and few

there be that find it. 15 Beware of false prophets, which come to you in sheep's clothing, but inwardly they are ravening wolves. 16 Ye shall know them by their fruits. Do men gather grapes of thorns, or figs of thistles? 17 Even so every good tree bringeth forth good fruit; but a corrupt tree bringeth forth evil fruit. 18 A good tree cannot bring forth evil fruit, neither can a corrupt tree bring forth good fruit. 19 Every tree that bringeth not forth good fruit is hewn down, and cast into the fire. 20 Wherefore by their fruits ye shall know them.

21 Not every one that saith unto me, Lord, Lord, shall enter into the kingdom of heaven; but he that doeth the will of my Father which is in heaven. 22 Many will say to me in that day, Lord, Lord, have we not prophesied in thy name? and in thy name have cast out devils? and in thy name done many wonderful works? 23 And then will I profess unto them, I never knew you: depart from me, ye that work iniquity. 24 Therefore whosoever heareth these sayings of mine, and doeth them, I will liken him unto a wise man, which built his house upon a rock: 25 And the rain descended, and the floods came, and the winds blew, and beat upon that house; and it fell not: for it was founded upon a rock. 26 And every one that heareth these sayings of mine, and doeth them not, shall be likened unto a foolish man, which built his house upon the sand: 27 And the rain descended, and the floods came, and the winds blew, and beat upon that house; and it fell: and great was the fall of it.

28 And it came to pass, when Jesus had ended these sayings, the people were astonished at his doctrine: 29 For he taught them as one having authority, and not as the scribes.

NOTES: MATTHEW CHAPTER 7

Discussion Point 4.6
Jesus has the Authority to Forgive Sins.
Son be of good cheer; thy sins be forgiven thee...Know that the Son of Man has power on earth to forgive sins. This claim, makes him equivalent with God; a claim that the Pharisees immediately consider blasphemy (Matt: 9:2-6).

✳✳✳

Matthew Chapter 9

1 And he entered into a ship, and passed over, and came into his own city.

2 And, behold, they brought to him a man sick of the palsy, lying on a bed: and Jesus seeing their faith said unto the sick of the palsy; *Son, be of good cheer; thy sins be forgiven thee.* 3 And, behold, certain of the scribes said within themselves, This man blasphemeth. 4 And Jesus knowing their thoughts said, *Wherefore think ye evil in your hearts? 5 For whether is easier, to say, Thy sins be forgiven thee; or to say, Arise, and walk? 6 But that ye may know that the Son of man hath power on earth to forgive sins,* (then saith he to the sick of the palsy,) *Arise, take up thy bed, and go unto thine house.*

7 And he arose, and departed to his house. 8 But when the multitudes saw it, they marvelled, and glorified God, which had given such power unto men. 9 And as Jesus passed forth from thence, he saw a man, named Matthew, sitting at the receipt of custom: and he saith unto him, *Follow me.* And he arose, and followed him. 10 And it came to pass, as Jesus sat at meat in the house, behold, many publicans and sinners came and sat down with him and his disciples. 11 And when the Pharisees saw it, they said unto his disciples, Why eateth your Master with publicans and sinners? 12 But when Jesus heard that, he said unto them, *They that be whole need not a physician, but they that are sick. 13 But go ye and learn what that meaneth, I will have mercy, and not sacrifice: for I am not come to call the righteous, but sinners to repentance.*

14 Then came to him the disciples of John, saying, Why do we and the Pharisees fast oft, but thy disciples fast not? 15 And Jesus said unto them, *Can the children of the bridechamber mourn, as long as the bridegroom is with them? but the days will come, when the bridegroom shall be taken from them, and then shall they*

HEALING PARALYSIS

fast. 16 *No man putteth a piece of new cloth unto an old garment, for that which is put in to fill it up taketh from the garment, and the rent is made worse.* 17 *Neither do men put new wine into old bottles: else the bottles break, and the wine runneth out, and the bottles perish: but they put new wine into new bottles, and both are preserved.*

18 While he spake these things unto them, behold, there came a certain ruler, and worshipped him, saying, My daughter is even now dead: but come and lay thy hand upon her, and she shall live. 19 And Jesus arose, and followed him, and so did his disciples. 20 And, behold, a woman, which was diseased with an issue of blood twelve years, came behind him, and touched the hem of his garment: 21 For she said within herself, If I may but touch his garment, I shall be whole. 22 But Jesus turned him about, and when he saw her, he said, *Daughter, be of good comfort; thy faith hath made thee whole.* And the woman was made whole from that hour. 23 And when Jesus came into the ruler's house, and saw the minstrels and the people making a noise, 24 He said unto them, *Give place: for the maid is not dead, but sleepeth.* And they laughed him to scorn. 25 But when the people were put forth, he went in, and took her by the hand, and the maid arose. 26 And the fame thereof went abroad into all that land. 27 And when Jesus departed thence, two blind men followed him, crying, and saying, Thou Son of David, have mercy on us. 28 And when he was come into the house, the blind men came to him: and Jesus saith unto them, *Believe ye that I am able to do this?* They said unto him, Yea, Lord. 29 Then touched he their eyes, saying, *According to your faith be it unto you.* 30 And their eyes were opened; and Jesus straitly charged them, saying, See that no man know it. 31 But they, when they were departed, spread abroad his fame in all that country. 32 As they went out, behold, they brought to him a dumb man possessed with a devil. 33 And when the devil was cast out, the dumb spake: and the multitudes marvelled, saying, It was never so seen in Israel. 34 But the Pharisees said, He casteth out devils through the prince of the devils.

35 And Jesus went about all the cities and villages, teaching in their synagogues, and preaching the gospel of the kingdom, and healing every sickness and every disease among the people. 36 But when he saw the multitudes, he was moved with compassion on them, because they fainted, and were scattered abroad, as sheep having no shepherd. 37 Then saith he unto his disciples, *The harvest truly is plenteous, but the labourers are few; 38 Pray ye therefore the Lord of the harvest, that he will send forth labourers into his harvest.*

NOTES: MATTHEW CHAPTER 9

Discussion Point 4.6
Jesus Declares in this Place there is one Greater than the Temple and that He is Lord of even the Sabbath day (Matt 12:6-8).

Discussion Point 4.7
Jesus speaks of the Deity of the Holy Ghost
Therefore I say unto you, All manner of sin and blasphemy shall be forgiven unto men; but the blasphemy against the Holy Ghost shall not be forgiven unto men.. And whosoever speaketh a work against the Son of man, it shall be forgiven him; but whosoever speaketh against the Holy Ghost, it shall not be forgiven him, neither in this world, neither in the world to come (Matt 12:31-32).

Discussion Point 4.8
Jesus foretells the Pharisees of His Death and 3 day burial as a sign (Matt 12:39-40).

***

Matthew Chapter 12

1 At that time Jesus went on the sabbath day through the corn; and his disciples were an hungred, and began to pluck the ears of corn, and to eat. 2 But when the Pharisees saw it, they said unto him, Behold, thy disciples do that which is not lawful to do upon the sabbath day. 3 But he said unto them, *Have ye not read what David did, when he was an hungred, and they that were with him; 4 How he entered into the house of God, and did eat the shewbread, which was not lawful for him to eat, neither for them which were with him, but only for the priests? 5 Or have ye not read in the law, how that on the sabbath days the priests in the temple profane the sabbath, and are blameless?*

6 But I say unto you, That in this place is one greater than the temple. 7 But if ye had known what this meaneth, I will have mercy, and not sacrifice, ye would not have condemned the guiltless. 8 For the Son of man is Lord even of the sabbath day.

9 And when he was departed thence, he went into their synagogue: 10 And, behold, there was a man which had his hand withered. And they asked him, saying, Is it lawful to heal on the sabbath days? that they might

accuse him. *11 And he said unto them, What man shall there be among you, that shall have one sheep, and if it fall into a pit on the sabbath day, will he not lay hold on it, and lift it out? 12 How much then is a man better than a sheep? Wherefore it is lawful to do well on the sabbath days. 13 Then saith he to the man, Stretch forth thine hand.* And he stretched it forth; and it was restored whole, like as the other. *14* Then the Pharisees went out, and held a council against him, how they might destroy him. *15* But when Jesus knew it, he withdrew himself from thence: and great multitudes followed him, and he healed them all; *16* And charged them that they should not make him known: *17* That it might be fulfilled which was spoken by Esaias the prophet, saying, *18* Behold my servant, whom I have chosen; my beloved, in whom my soul is well pleased: I will put my spirit upon him, and he shall shew judgment to the Gentiles. *19* He shall not strive, nor cry; neither shall any man hear his voice in the streets. *20* A bruised reed shall he not break, and smoking flax shall he not quench, till he send forth judgment unto victory. *21* And in his name shall the Gentiles trust. *22* Then was brought unto him one possessed with a devil, blind, and dumb: and he healed him, insomuch that the blind and dumb both spake and saw. *23* And all the people were amazed, and said, Is not this the son of David? *24* But when the Pharisees heard it, they said, This fellow doth not cast out devils, but by Beelzebub the prince of the devils. *25* And Jesus knew their thoughts, and said unto them, *Every kingdom divided against itself is brought to desolation; and every city or house divided against itself shall not stand: 26 And if Satan cast out Satan, he is divided against himself; how shall then his kingdom stand? 27 And if I by Beelzebub cast out devils, by whom do your children cast them out? therefore they shall be your judges. 28 But if I cast out devils by the Spirit of God, then the kingdom of God is come unto you. 29 Or else how can one enter into a strong man's house, and spoil his goods, except he first bind the strong man? and then he will spoil his house.*

> *30 He that is not with me is against me; and he that gathereth not with me scattereth abroad. 31 Wherefore I say unto you, All manner of sin and blasphemy shall be forgiven unto men: but the blasphemy against the Holy Ghost shall not be forgiven unto men. 32 And whosoever speaketh a word against the Son of man, it shall be forgiven him: but whosoever speaketh against the Holy Ghost, it shall not be forgiven him, neither in this world, neither in the world to come.*

HEALING PARALYSIS

33 Either make the tree good, and his fruit good; or else make the tree corrupt, and his fruit corrupt: for the tree is known by his fruit. 34 O generation of vipers, how can ye, being evil, speak good things? for out of the abundance of the heart the mouth speaketh. 35 A good man out of the good treasure of the heart bringeth forth good things: and an evil man out of the evil treasure bringeth forth evil things. 36 But I say unto you, That every idle word that men shall speak, they shall give account thereof in the day of judgment. 37 For by thy words thou shalt be justified, and by thy words thou shalt be condemned. 38 Then certain of the scribes and of the Pharisees answered, saying, Master, we would see a sign from thee.

39 But he answered and said unto them, *An evil and adulterous generation seeketh after a sign; and there shall no sign be given to it, but the sign of the prophet Jonas: 40 For as Jonas was three days and three nights in the whale's belly; so shall the Son of man be three days and three nights in the heart of the earth.*

41 The men of Nineveh shall rise in judgment with this generation, and shall condemn it: because they repented at the preaching of Jonas; and, behold, a greater than Jonas is here. 42 The queen of the south shall rise up in the judgment with this generation, and shall condemn it: for she came from the uttermost parts of the earth to hear the wisdom of Solomon; and, behold, a greater than Solomon is here. 43 When the unclean spirit is gone out of a man, he walketh through dry places, seeking rest, and findeth none. 44 Then he saith, I will return into my house from whence I came out; and when he is come, he findeth it empty, swept, and garnished. 45 Then goeth he, and taketh with himself seven other spirits more wicked than himself, and they enter in and dwell there: and the last state of that man is worse than the first. Even so shall it be also unto this wicked generation. 46 While he yet talked to the people, behold, his mother and his brethren stood without, desiring to speak with him. 47 Then one said unto him, Behold, thy mother and thy brethren stand without, desiring to speak with thee. 48 But he answered and said unto him that told him, *Who is my mother? and who are my brethren?* 49 And he stretched forth his hand toward his disciples, and said, *Behold my mother and my brethren! 50 For whosoever shall do the will of my Father which is in heaven, the same is my brother, and sister, and mother.*

NOTES: MATTHEW CHAPTER 12

Discussion Point 4.9
Jesus Declaration that He is the Christ
Jesus asked the Disciples "Whom do men say that I, the Son of Man am?...But whom do ye say that I am? When Peter responded with "Thou art the Christ the Son of the Living God" Jesus' reply confirms Peter's declaration saying " Blessed art thou...for flesh and blood have not revealed it unto thee, but my Father which is in heaven...And I say also unto thee..I will give unto thee, the keys of the kingdom of heaven, and whatsoever though shalt bind on earth, shall be bound in heaven...... For the Son of man shall come in the glory of his Father with his angels; and then he shall reward every man according to his works" (Matt 16:13-28).

***

Matthew Chapter 16

1 The Pharisees also with the Sadducees came, and tempting desired him that he would shew them a sign from heaven. *2* He answered and said unto them, *When it is evening, ye say, It will be fair weather: for the sky is red. 3 And in the morning, It will be foul weather to day: for the sky is red and lowring. O ye hypocrites, ye can discern the face of the sky; but can ye not discern the signs of the times? 4 A wicked and adulterous generation seeketh after a sign; and there shall no sign be given unto it, but the sign of the prophet Jonas.* And he left them, and departed.

5 And when his disciples were come to the other side, they had forgotten to take bread. *6* Then Jesus said unto them, *Take heed and beware of the leaven of the Pharisees and of the Sadducees.* 7 And they reasoned among themselves, saying, It is because we have taken no bread. *8* Which when Jesus perceived, he said unto them, *O ye of little faith, why reason ye among yourselves, because ye have brought no bread? 9 Do ye not yet understand, neither remember the five loaves of the five thousand, and how many baskets ye took up? 10 Neither the seven loaves of the four thousand, and how many baskets ye took up? 11 How is it that ye do not understand that I spake it not to you concerning bread, that ye should beware of the leaven of the Pharisees and of the Sadducees?* 12 Then understood they how that he bade them not beware of the leaven of bread, but of the doctrine of the Pharisees and of the Sadducees.

13 When Jesus came into the coasts of Caesarea Philippi, he asked his disciples, saying, *Whom do men say that I the Son of man am?* 14 And they said, Some say that thou art John the Baptist:

some, Elias; and others, Jeremias, or one of the prophets. *15* He saith unto them, *But whom say ye that I am?* *16* And Simon Peter answered and said, Thou art the Christ, the Son of the living God. *17* And Jesus answered and said unto him, *Blessed art thou, Simon Barjona: for flesh and blood hath not revealed it unto thee, but my Father which is in heaven. 18 And I say also unto thee, That thou art Peter, and upon this rock I will build my church; and the gates of hell shall not prevail against it. 19 And I will give unto thee the keys of the kingdom of heaven: and whatsoever thou shalt bind on earth shall be bound in heaven: and whatsoever thou shalt loose on earth shall be loosed in heaven.* *20* Then charged he his disciples that they should tell no man that he was Jesus the Christ.

21 From that time forth began Jesus to shew unto his disciples, how that he must go unto Jerusalem, and suffer many things of the elders and chief priests and scribes, and be killed, and be raised again the third day. *22* Then Peter took him, and began to rebuke him, saying, Be it far from thee, Lord: this shall not be unto thee. *23* But he turned, and said unto Peter, *Get thee behind me, Satan: thou art an offence unto me: for thou savourest not the things that be of God, but those that be of men.*

24 Then said Jesus unto his disciples, *If any man will come after me, let him deny himself, and take up his cross, and follow me. 25 For whosoever will save his life shall lose it: and whosoever will lose his life for my sake shall find it. 26 For what is a man profited, if he shall gain the whole world, and lose his own soul? or what shall a man give in exchange for his soul? 27 For the Son of man shall come in the glory of his Father with his angels; and then he shall reward every man according to his works. 28 Verily I say unto you, There be some standing here, which shall not taste of death, till they see the Son of man coming in his kingdom.*

NOTES: MATTHEW CHAPTER 16

Discussion Point 4.10
Jesus Warns Disciples against False Prophets and against trying to Predict the End of the World
Take heed that no man deceive you...For many shall come in my name saying I am Christ; and shall deceive many...and many false prophets shall rise and shall deceive many (Matt 24:4-12).

***

Matthew Chapter 24

1 And Jesus went out, and departed from the temple: and his disciples came to him for to shew him the buildings of the temple. 2 And Jesus said unto them, *See ye not all these things? verily I say unto you, There shall not be left here one stone upon another, that shall not be thrown down.* 3 And as he sat upon the mount of Olives, the disciples came unto him privately, saying, Tell us, when shall these things be? and what shall be the sign of thy coming, and of the end of the world?

> **4 And Jesus answered and said unto them,** *Take heed that no man deceive you. 5 For many shall come in my name, saying, I am Christ; and shall deceive many. 6 And ye shall hear of wars and rumours of wars: see that ye be not troubled: for all these things must come to pass, but the end is not yet. 7 For nation shall rise against nation, and kingdom against kingdom: and there shall be famines, and pestilences, and earthquakes, in divers places. 8 All these are the beginning of sorrows. 9 Then shall they deliver you up to be afflicted, and shall kill you: and ye shall be hated of all nations for my name's sake. 10 And then shall many be offended, and shall betray one another, and shall hate one another. 11 And many false prophets shall rise, and shall deceive many. 12 And because iniquity shall abound, the love of many shall wax cold. 13 But he that shall endure unto the end, the same shall be saved.*

14 And this gospel of the kingdom shall be preached in all the world for a witness unto all nations; and then shall the end come. 15 When ye therefore shall see the abomination of desolation, spoken of by Daniel the prophet, stand in the holy place, (whoso readeth, let him understand:) 16 Then let them which be in Judaea flee into the mountains: 17 Let him which

HEALING PARALYSIS

is on the housetop not come down to take any thing out of his house: 18 Neither let him which is in the field return back to take his clothes. 19 And woe unto them that are with child, and to them that give suck in those days! 20 But pray ye that your flight be not in the winter, neither on the sabbath day: 21 For then shall be great tribulation, such as was not since the beginning of the world to this time, no, nor ever shall be. 22 And except those days should be shortened, there should no flesh be saved: but for the elect's sake those days shall be shortened. 23 Then if any man shall say unto you, Lo, here is Christ, or there; believe it not. 24 For there shall arise false Christs, and false prophets, and shall shew great signs and wonders; insomuch that, if it were possible, they shall deceive the very elect. 25 Behold, I have told you before. 26 Wherefore if they shall say unto you, Behold, he is in the desert; go not forth: behold, he is in the secret chambers; believe it not. 27 For as the lightning cometh out of the east, and shineth even unto the west; so shall also the coming of the Son of man be. 28 For wheresoever the carcase is, there will the eagles be gathered together. 29 Immediately after the tribulation of those days shall the sun be darkened, and the moon shall not give her light, and the stars shall fall from heaven, and the powers of the heavens shall be shaken: 30 And then shall appear the sign of the Son of man in heaven: and then shall all the tribes of the earth mourn, and they shall see the Son of man coming in the clouds of heaven with power and great glory. 31 And he shall send his angels with a great sound of a trumpet, and they shall gather together his elect from the four winds, from one end of heaven to the other.

32 Now learn a parable of the fig tree; When his branch is yet tender, and putteth forth leaves, ye know that summer is nigh: 33 So likewise ye, when ye shall see all these things, know that it is near, even at the doors. 34 Verily I say unto you, This generation shall not pass, till all these things be fulfilled. 35 Heaven and earth shall pass away, but my words shall not pass away. 36 But of that day and hour knoweth no man, no, not the angels of heaven, but my Father only. 37 But as the days of Noe were, so shall also the coming of the Son of man be. 38 For as in the days that were before the flood they were eating and drinking, marrying and giving in marriage, until the day that Noe entered into the ark, 39 And knew not until the flood came, and took them all away; so shall also the coming of the Son of man be. 40 Then shall two be in the field; the one shall be taken, and the other left. 41 Two women shall be grinding at the mill; the one shall be taken, and the other left. 42 Watch therefore: for ye know not what hour your Lord doth come. 43 But know this, that if the goodman of the house had known in what watch the thief would come, he would have watched, and would not have suffered his house to be broken up. 44 Therefore be ye also ready: for in such an hour as ye think not the Son of man cometh. 45 Who then is a faithful and wise servant, whom his lord hath made ruler over his household, to give them meat in due season? 46 Blessed is that servant, whom his lord when he cometh shall find so doing. 47 Verily I say unto you, That he shall make him ruler over all his goods. 48 But and if that evil servant shall say in his heart,

My lord delayeth his coming; 49 And shall begin to smite his fellowservants, and to eat and drink with the drunken; 50 The lord of that servant shall come in a day when he looketh not for him, and in an hour that he is not aware of, 51 And shall cut him asunder, and appoint him his portion with the hypocrites: there shall be weeping and gnashing of teeth.

NOTES: MATTHEW CHAPTER 24

Discussion Point 4.11
After His death and resurrection, Jesus instructs the Disciples to make followers, Baptizing them in the name of the "Father, Son and Holy Ghost." This is often referred to by Christians as the "Holy Trinity" (Matt. 28:18-20).

※※※

Matthew Chapter 28

1 In the end of the sabbath, as it began to dawn toward the first day of the week, came Mary Magdalene and the other Mary to see the sepulchre. *2* And, behold, there was a great earthquake: for the angel of the Lord descended from heaven, and came and rolled back the stone from the door, and sat upon it. *3* His countenance was like lightning, and his raiment white as snow: *4* And for fear of him the keepers did shake, and became as dead men. *5* And the angel answered and said unto the women, Fear not ye: for I know that ye seek Jesus, which was crucified. *6* He is not here: for he is risen, as he said. Come, see the place where the Lord lay. *7* And go quickly, and tell his disciples that he is risen from the dead; and, behold, he goeth before you into Galilee; there shall ye see him: lo, I have told you. *8* And they departed quickly from the sepulchre with fear and great joy; and did run to bring his disciples word. *9* And as they went to tell his disciples, behold, Jesus met them, saying, *All hail.* And they came and held him by the feet, and worshipped him. *10* Then said Jesus unto them, *Be not afraid: go tell my brethren that they go into Galilee, and there shall they see me.* *11* Now when they were going, behold, some of the watch came into the city, and shewed unto the chief priests all the things that were done. *12* And when they were assembled with the elders, and had taken counsel, they gave large money unto the soldiers, *13* Saying, Say ye, His disciples came by night, and stole him away while we slept. *14* And if this come to the governor's ears, we will persuade him, and secure you. *15* So they took the money, and did as they were taught: and this saying is commonly reported among the Jews until this day. *16* Then the eleven disciples went away into Galilee, into a mountain where Jesus had appointed them. *17* And when they saw him, they worshipped him: but some doubted.

HEALING PARALYSIS

18 And Jesus came and spake unto them, saying, *All power is given unto me in heaven and in earth. 19 Go ye therefore, and teach all nations, baptizing them in the name of the Father, and of the Son, and of the Holy Ghost: 20 Teaching them to observe all things whatsoever I have commanded you: and, lo, I am with you alway, even unto the end of the world.* Amen.

NOTES: MATTHEW CHAPTER 28

Discussion Point 4.12
Jesus informs Nicodemus that he must be "born again" to enter the Kingdom of God (John 3:3-7).

Discussion Point 4:13
Jesus Describes that He was Sent into the World as God's Begotten Son to save it
God so loved the world that he gave his only begotten Son, that whoeverso believes in him shall have eternal life (John 3:12-16).

***

John Chapter 3

1 There was a man of the Pharisees, named Nicodemus, a ruler of the Jews: 2 The same came to Jesus by night, and said unto him, Rabbi, we know that thou art a teacher come from God: for no man can do these miracles that thou doest, except God be with him.

3 Jesus answered and said unto him, Verily, verily, I say unto thee, Except a man be born again, he cannot see the kingdom of God. 4 Nicodemus saith unto him, How can a man be born when he is old? can he enter the second time into his mother's womb, and be born? 5 Jesus answered, Verily, verily, I say unto thee, Except a man be born of water and of the Spirit, he cannot enter into the kingdom of God. 6 That which is born of the flesh is flesh; and that which is born of the Spirit is spirit. 7 Marvel not that I said unto thee, Ye must be born again.

8 The wind bloweth where it listeth, and thou hearest the sound thereof, but canst not tell whence it cometh, and whither it goeth: so is every one that is born of the Spirit. 9 Nicodemus answered and said unto him, How can these things be? 10 Jesus answered and said unto him, Art thou a master of Israel, and knowest not these things? 11 Verily, verily, I say unto thee, We speak that we do know, and testify that we have seen; and ye receive not our witness.

12 If I have told you earthly things, and ye believe not, how shall ye believe, if I tell you of heavenly things? 13 And no man hath ascended up to heaven, but he that came down from heaven, even the Son of man which is in heaven. 14 And as Moses lifted up the serpent in the wilderness, even so must the Son of man be lifted up: 15 That whosoever believeth in him should not perish, but have eternal life. 16 For God so loved the world, that he gave his only begotten Son, that whosoever believeth in him should not perish, but have everlasting life. 17 For God sent not his Son into the world to condemn the world; but that the world through him might be saved. 18 He that believeth on him is not condemned: but he that believeth not is condemned already, because he hath not believed in the name of the only begotten Son of God.

19 And this is the condemnation, that light is come into the world, and men loved darkness rather than light, because their deeds were evil. 20 For every one that doeth evil hateth the light, neither cometh to the light, lest his deeds should be reproved. 21 But he that doeth truth cometh to the light, that his deeds may be made manifest, that they are wrought in God. 22 After these things came Jesus and his disciples into the land of Judaea; and there he tarried with them, and baptized. 23 And John also was baptizing in Aenon near to Salim, because there was much water there: and they came, and were baptized. 24 For John was not yet cast into prison. 25 Then there arose a question between some of John's disciples and the Jews about purifying. 26 And they came unto John, and said unto him, Rabbi, he that was with thee beyond Jordan, to whom thou barest witness, behold, the same baptizeth, and all men come to him. 27 John answered and said, A man can receive nothing, except it be given him from heaven. 28 Ye yourselves bear me witness, that I said, I am not the Christ, but that I am sent before him. 29 He that hath the bride is the bridegroom: but the friend of the bridegroom, which standeth and heareth him, rejoiceth greatly because of the bridegroom's voice: this my joy therefore is fulfilled. 30 He must increase, but I must decrease. 31 He that cometh from above is above all: he that is of the earth is earthly, and speaketh of the earth: he that cometh from heaven is above all. 32 And what he hath seen and heard, that he testifieth; and no man receiveth his testimony. 33 He that hath received his testimony hath set to his seal that God is true. 34 For he whom God hath sent speaketh the words of God: for God giveth not the Spirit by measure unto him. 35 The Father loveth the Son, and hath given all things into his hand. 36 He that believeth on the Son hath everlasting life: and he that believeth not the Son shall not see life; but the wrath of God abideth on him.

NOTES: JOHN CHAPTER 3

Discussion Point 4.14
Jesus Declares that he has Authority for all Judgment
For the Father judgeth no man but hath committed all judgment unto the Son... That all men should honor the Son, even as they honor the Father. He that honoreth not the Son, honoreth, not the Father which hath sent him (John 5:17-27).

***

John Chapter 5

1 After this there was a feast of the Jews; and Jesus went up to Jerusalem. 2 Now there is at Jerusalem by the sheep market a pool, which is called in the Hebrew tongue Bethesda, having five porches. 3 In these lay a great multitude of impotent folk, of blind, halt, withered, waiting for the moving of the water. 4 For an angel went down at a certain season into the pool, and troubled the water: whosoever then first after the troubling of the water stepped in was made whole of whatsoever disease he had. 5 And a certain man was there, which had an infirmity thirty and eight years. 6 When Jesus saw him lie, and knew that he had been now a long time in that case, he saith unto him, *Wilt thou be made whole?* 7 The impotent man answered him, Sir, I have no man, when the water is troubled, to put me into the pool: but while I am coming, another steppeth down before me. 8 Jesus saith unto him, *Rise, take up thy bed, and walk.* 9 And immediately the man was made whole, and took up his bed, and walked: and on the same day was the sabbath. 10 The Jews therefore said unto him that was cured, It is the sabbath day: it is not lawful for thee to carry thy bed. 11 He answered them, He that made me whole, the same said unto me, *Take up thy bed, and walk.* 12 Then asked they him, What man is that which said unto thee, Take up thy bed, and walk? 13 And he that was healed wist not who it was: for Jesus had conveyed himself away, a multitude being in that place. 14 Afterward Jesus findeth him in the temple, and said unto him, *Behold, thou art made whole: sin no more, lest a worse thing come unto thee.* 15 The man departed, and told the Jews that it was Jesus, which had made him whole. 16 And therefore did the Jews persecute Jesus, and sought to slay him, because he had done these things on the sabbath day.

17 But Jesus answered them, *My Father worketh hitherto, and I work.* 18 Therefore the Jews sought the more to kill him, because he

HEALING PARALYSIS

not only had broken the sabbath, but said also that God was his Father, making himself equal with God. *19 Then answered Jesus and said unto them, Verily, verily, I say unto you, The Son can do nothing of himself, but what he seeth the Father do: for what things soever he doeth, these also doeth the Son likewise. 20 For the Father loveth the Son, and sheweth him all things that himself doeth: and he will shew him greater works than these, that ye may marvel. 21 For as the Father raiseth up the dead, and quickeneth them; even so the Son quickeneth whom he will. 22 For the Father judgeth no man, but hath committed all judgment unto the Son: 23 That all men should honour the Son, even as they honour the Father. He that honoureth not the Son honoureth not the Father which hath sent him. 24 Verily, verily, I say unto you, He that heareth my word, and believeth on him that sent me, hath everlasting life, and shall not come into condemnation; but is passed from death unto life. 25 Verily, verily, I say unto you, The hour is coming, and now is, when the dead shall hear the voice of the Son of God: and they that hear shall live. 26 For as the Father hath life in himself; so hath he given to the Son to have life in himself; 27 And hath given him authority to execute judgment also, because he is the Son of man.*

28 Marvel not at this: for the hour is coming, in the which all that are in the graves shall hear his voice, 29 And shall come forth; they that have done good, unto the resurrection of life; and they that have done evil, unto the resurrection of damnation. 30 I can of mine own self do nothing: as I hear, I judge: and my judgment is just; because I seek not mine own will, but the will of the Father which hath sent me. 31 If I bear witness of myself, my witness is not true. 32 There is another that beareth witness of me; and I know that the witness which he witnesseth of me is true. 33 Ye sent unto John, and he bare witness unto the truth. 34 But I receive not testimony from man: but these things I say, that ye might be saved. 35 He was a burning and a shining light: and ye were willing for a season to rejoice in his light. 36 But I have greater witness than that of John: for the works which the Father hath given me to finish, the same works that I do, bear witness of me, that the Father hath sent me. 37 And the Father himself, which hath sent me, hath borne witness of me. Ye have neither heard his voice at any time, nor seen his shape. 38 And ye have not his word abiding in you: for whom he hath sent, him ye believe not. 39 Search the scriptures; for in them ye think ye have eternal life: and they are they which testify of me. 40 And ye will not come to me, that ye might have life. 41 I receive not honour from men. 42 But I know you, that ye have not the love of God in you. 43 I am come in my Father's name, and ye receive me not: if another shall come in his own name, him ye will receive. 44 How can ye believe, which receive honour one of another, and seek not the honour that cometh from God only? 45 Do not think that I will accuse you to the Father: there is one that accuseth you, even Moses, in whom ye trust. 46 For had ye believed Moses, ye would have believed me: for he wrote of me. 47 But if ye believe not his writings, how shall ye believe my words?

NOTES: JOHN CHAPTER 5

Discussion Point 4.14

Jesus declaration that the Father draws men unto him, and that He is the Manna from Heaven.

Note the necessity of acceptance of Christ to receive salvation as Jesus proclaims "No man can come to me, except the Father which hath sent me draw him; and I will raise him up at the last day....He that believeth on me hath everlasting life...I am the living bread which came down from heaven; if any man eat of this bread, he shall live forever and the bread that I will give, is my flesh, which I will give for the life of the world...Except ye eat the flesh of the Son of man and drink his blood, ye have no life in you" (John 6:32-51).

***

<u>John Chapter 6</u>

1 After these things Jesus went over the sea of Galilee, which is the sea of Tiberias. *2* And a great multitude followed him, because they saw his miracles which he did on them that were diseased. *3* And Jesus went up into a mountain, and there he sat with his disciples. *4* And the passover, a feast of the Jews, was nigh. *5* When Jesus then lifted up his eyes, and saw a great company come unto him, he saith unto Philip, *Whence shall we buy bread, that these may eat?* *6* And this he said to prove him: for he himself knew what he would do. *7* Philip answered him, Two hundred pennyworth of bread is not sufficient for them, that every one of them may take a little. *8* One of his disciples, Andrew, Simon Peter's brother, saith unto him, *9* There is a lad here, which hath five barley loaves, and two small fishes: but what are they among so many? *10* And Jesus said, *Make the men sit down.* Now there was much grass in the place. So the men sat down, in number about five thousand. *11* And Jesus took the loaves; and when he had given thanks, he distributed to the disciples, and the disciples to them that were set down; and likewise of the fishes as much as they would. *12* When they were filled, he said unto his disciples, *Gather up the fragments that remain, that nothing be lost.* *13* Therefore they gathered them together, and filled twelve baskets with the fragments of the five barley loaves, which remained over and above unto them that had eaten. *14* Then those men, when they had seen the miracle that Jesus did, said, This is of a truth that prophet that should come into the world.

HEALING PARALYSIS

15 When Jesus therefore perceived that they would come and take him by force, to make him a king, he departed again into a mountain himself alone. *16* And when even was now come, his disciples went down unto the sea, *17* And entered into a ship, and went over the sea toward Capernaum. And it was now dark, and Jesus was not come to them. *18* And the sea arose by reason of a great wind that blew. *19* So when they had rowed about five and twenty or thirty furlongs, they see Jesus walking on the sea, and drawing nigh unto the ship: and they were afraid. *20* But he saith unto them, *It is I; be not afraid.* *21* Then they willingly received him into the ship: and immediately the ship was at the land whither they went. *22* The day following, when the people which stood on the other side of the sea saw that there was none other boat there, save that one whereinto his disciples were entered, and that Jesus went not with his disciples into the boat, but that his disciples were gone away alone; *23* (Howbeit there came other boats from Tiberias nigh unto the place where they did eat bread, after that the Lord had given thanks:) *24* When the people therefore saw that Jesus was not there, neither his disciples, they also took shipping, and came to Capernaum, seeking for Jesus. *25* And when they had found him on the other side of the sea, they said unto him, Rabbi, when camest thou hither? *26* Jesus answered them and said, *Verily, verily, I say unto you, Ye seek me, not because ye saw the miracles, but because ye did eat of the loaves, and were filled. 27 Labour not for the meat which perisheth, but for that meat which endureth unto everlasting life, which the Son of man shall give unto you: for him hath God the Father sealed.* *28* Then said they unto him, What shall we do, that we might work the works of God? *29* Jesus answered and said unto them, *This is the work of God, that ye believe on him whom he hath sent.* *30* They said therefore unto him, What sign shewest thou then, that we may see, and believe thee? what dost thou work? *31* Our fathers did eat manna in the desert; as it is written, He gave them bread from heaven to eat.

32 **Then Jesus said unto them,** *Verily, verily, I say unto you, Moses gave you not that bread from heaven; but my Father giveth you the true bread from heaven. 33 For the bread of God is he which cometh down from heaven, and giveth life unto the world.* **34 Then said they unto him, Lord, evermore give us this bread. 35 And Jesus said unto them,** *I am the bread of life: he that cometh to me shall never hunger; and he that believeth on me shall never thirst. 36 But I said unto you, That ye also* *have seen me, and believe not. 37 All that the Father giveth me shall come to me; and him that cometh to me I will in no wise cast out. 38 For I came down from heaven, not to do mine own will, but the will of him that sent me. 39 And this is the Father's will which hath sent me, that of all which he hath given me I should lose nothing, but should raise it up again at the last day. 40 And this is the will of him that sent me, that every one which seeth the Son, and believeth on him, may have everlasting life: and I will raise him up at the last day.*

41 The Jews then murmured at him, because he said, I am the bread which came down from heaven. 42 And they said, Is not this Jesus, the son of Joseph, whose father and mother we know? how is it then that he saith, I came down from heaven? 43 Jesus therefore answered and said unto them, Murmur not among yourselves.

44 No man can come to me, except the Father which hath sent me draw him: and I will raise him up at the last day. 45 It is written in the prophets, And they shall be all taught of God. Every man therefore that hath heard, and hath learned of the Father, cometh unto me. 46 Not that any man hath seen the Father, save he which is of God, he hath seen the Father. 47 Verily, verily, I say unto you, He that believeth on me hath everlasting life. 48 I am that bread of life. 49 Your fathers did eat manna in the wilderness, and are dead. 50 This is the bread which cometh down from heaven, that a man may eat thereof, and not die. 51 I am the living bread which came down from heaven: if any man eat of this bread, he shall live for ever: and the bread that I will give is my flesh, which I will give for the life of the world.

52 The Jews therefore strove among themselves, saying, How can this man give us his flesh to eat? 53 Then Jesus said unto them, *Verily, verily, I say unto you, Except ye eat the flesh of the Son of man, and drink his blood, ye have no life in you. 54 Whoso eateth my flesh, and drinketh my blood, hath eternal life; and I will raise him up at the last day. 55 For my flesh is meat indeed, and my blood is drink indeed. 56 He that eateth my flesh, and drinketh my blood, dwelleth in me, and I in him. 57 As the living Father hath sent me, and I live by the Father: so he that eateth me, even he shall live by me. 58 This is that bread which came down from heaven: not as your fathers did eat manna, and are dead: he that eateth of this bread shall live for ever.* 59 These things said he in the synagogue, as he taught in Capernaum.

60 Many therefore of his disciples, when they had heard this, said, This is an hard saying; who can hear it? *61* When Jesus knew in himself that his disciples murmured at it, he said unto them, *Doth this offend you? 62 What and if ye shall see the Son of man ascend up where he was before? 63 It is the spirit that quickeneth; the flesh profiteth nothing: the words that I speak unto you, they are spirit, and they are life. 64 But there are some of you that believe not.* For Jesus knew from the beginning who they were that believed not, and who should betray him. *65* And he said, *Therefore said I unto you, that no man can come unto me, except it were given unto him of my Father.* 66 From that time many of his disciples went back, and walked no more with him. *67* Then said Jesus unto the twelve, *Will ye also go away?* 68 Then Simon Peter answered him, Lord, to whom shall we go? thou hast the words of eternal life. *69* And we believe and are sure that thou art that Christ, the Son of the living God. *70* Jesus answered them, *Have not I chosen you twelve, and one of you is a devil?* 71 He spake of Judas Iscariot the son of Simon: for he it was that should betray him, being one of the twelve.

NOTES: JOHN CHAPTER 6

Discussion Point 4.15
Jesus declares that they who have seen Him has seen the Father.
During the last supper before His betrayal, Jesus again informs the disciples that he must leave them. The disciples wishing Jesus to remain, begin to implore him not to go. Jesus replies with the necessity of his departure. Note in the first portion of the chapter, Jesus identifies himself as being one with the Father, that no man comes to the Father except by Him, and that anything asked in His (Jesus) name will He do, that the Father will be glorified in the Son (John 14:1-14).

Discussion Point 4.16
Jesus will Send a Comforter, The Holy Ghost
Here Jesus tells the disciples that he will send a comforter after he departs. "And I will pray the Father and he shall give you another Comforter that he may abide with you forever...Even the Spirit of truth; whom the work cannot receive, because it seeth him not, neither knoweth him, but ye know him for he dwelleth with you, and shall be in you. I will not leave you comfortless: I will come to you Yet a little while and the world seeth me no more; but ye see me, because I live, ye shall live also. At that day ye shall know that I am in my Father, and ye in me, and I in you. But the Comforter which is the Holy Ghost whom the Father will send in my name, he shall teach you all things, and bring all things to your remembrance, whatsoever I have said unto you" (John 14:15-26).

✽✽✽

<u>John Chapter 14</u>

1 Let not your heart be troubled: ye believe in God, believe also in me. 2 In my Father's house are many mansions: if it were not so, I would have told you. I go to prepare a place for you. 3 And if I go and prepare a place for you, I will come again, and receive you unto myself; that where I am, there ye may be also.
4 And whither I go ye know, and the way ye know. 5 Thomas saith unto him, Lord, we know not whither thou goest; and how can we know the way? 6 Jesus saith unto him, I am the way, the truth, and the life: no man cometh unto the Father, but by me. 7 If ye had known me, ye should have known my Father also: and from henceforth ye know him, and have seen him. 8 Philip saith unto him, Lord, shew us the

Father, and it sufficeth us. 9 Jesus saith unto him, *Have I been so long time with you, and yet hast thou not known me, Philip? he that hath seen me hath seen the Father; and how sayest thou then, Shew us the Father? 10 Believest thou not that I am in the Father, and the Father in me? the words that I speak unto you I speak not of myself: but the Father that dwelleth in me, he doeth the works. 11 Believe me that I am in the Father, and the Father in me: or else believe me for the very works' sake. 12 Verily, verily, I say unto you, He that believeth on me, the works that I do shall he do also; and greater works than these shall he do; because I go unto my Father. 13 And whatsoever ye shall ask in my name, that will I do, that the Father may be glorified in the Son. 14 If ye shall ask any thing in my name, I will do it.*

15 If ye love me, keep my commandments. 16 And I will pray the Father, and he shall give you another Comforter, that he may abide with you for ever; 17 Even the Spirit of truth; whom the world cannot receive, because it seeth him not, neither knoweth him: but ye know him; for he dwelleth with you, and shall be in you. 18 I will not leave you comfortless: I will come to you. 19 Yet a little while, and the world seeth me no more; but ye see me: because I live, ye shall live also. 20 At that day ye shall know that I am in my Father, and ye in me, and I in you. 21 He that hath my commandments, and keepeth them, he it is that loveth me: and he that loveth me shall be loved of my Father, and I will love him, and will manifest myself to him. 22 Judas saith unto him, not Iscariot, Lord, how is it that thou wilt manifest thyself unto us, and not unto the world? 23 Jesus answered and said unto him, If a man love me, he will keep my words: and my Father will love him, and we will come unto him, and make our abode with him. 24 He that loveth me not keepeth not my sayings: and the word which ye hear is not mine, but the Father's which sent me.

25 These things have I spoken unto you, being yet present with you. 26 But the Comforter, which is the Holy Ghost, whom the Father will send in my name, he shall teach you all things, and bring all things to your remembrance, whatsoever I have said unto you.

27 Peace I leave with you, my peace I give unto you: not as the world giveth, give I unto you. Let not your heart be troubled, neither let it be afraid. 28 Ye have heard how I said unto you, I go away, and come again unto you. If ye loved me, ye would rejoice, because I said, I go unto the Father: for my Father is greater than I. 29 And now I have told you

HEALING PARALYSIS

before it come to pass, that, when it is come to pass, ye might believe. 30 Hereafter I will not talk much with you: for the prince of this world cometh, and hath nothing in me. 31 But that the world may know that I love the Father; and as the Father gave me commandment, even so I do. Arise, let us go hence.

NOTES: JOHN CHAPTER 14

Discussion Point 4.17
The Holy Ghost will Glorify Jesus and the Father
Jesus Proclaims *"Nevertheless I tell you the truth. It is expedient for you that I go away, for if I go not away, the Comforter will not come unto you. And when he is come he will reprove the world of sin and of righteousness and of judgment. He shall glorify me: for he shall receive of mine, and shall shew it unto you. All things that the Father hath are mine: therefore said I, that he shall take of mine, and shall shew it unto you"* (John 16: 7-15).

Discussion Point 4.18
When you Ask in Jesus Name, you are Praying Directly to the Father
In the final moments before Jesus is betrayed, the disciples finally "get it." With this, Jesus proclaims that when they pray in His name, he will no longer have to pray to the Father on their behalf, because the Father himself loveth those who love Jesus. (John 16:23-27).

***

John Chapter 16

1 These things have I spoken unto you, that ye should not be offended. 2 They shall put you out of the synagogues: yea, the time cometh, that whosoever killeth you will think that he doeth God service. 3 And these things will they do unto you, because they have not known the Father, nor me. 4 But these things have I told you, that when the time shall come, ye may remember that I told you of them. And these things I said not unto you at the beginning, because I was with you. 5 But now I go my way to him that sent me; and none of you asketh me, Whither goest thou? 6 But because I have said these things unto you, sorrow hath filled your heart.

7 Nevertheless I tell you the truth; It is expedient for you that I go away: for if I go not away, the Comforter will not come unto you; but if I depart, I will send him unto you. 8 And when he is come, he will reprove the world of sin, and of righteousness, and of judgment: 9 Of sin, because they believe not on me; 10 Of righteousness, because I go to my Father, and ye see me no more; 11 Of judgment, because the prince of this world is judged. 12 I have yet many things to say unto you, but ye cannot bear them now. 13 Howbeit when he, the Spirit of truth, is come, he will guide you into all truth: for he shall not speak of himself; but whatsoever he shall hear, that

shall he speak: and he will shew you things to come. 14 He shall glorify me: for he shall receive of mine, and shall shew it unto you. 15 All things that the Father hath are mine: therefore said I, that he shall take of mine, and shall shew it unto you.

16 A little while, and ye shall not see me: and again, a little while, and ye shall see me, because I go to the Father. 17 Then said some of his disciples among themselves, What is this that he saith unto us, A little while, and ye shall not see me: and again, a little while, and ye shall see me: and, Because I go to the Father? 18 They said therefore, What is this that he saith, A little while? we cannot tell what he saith. 19 Now Jesus knew that they were desirous to ask him, and said unto them, Do ye enquire among yourselves of that I said, A little while, and ye shall not see me: and again, a little while, and ye shall see me? 20 Verily, verily, I say unto you, That ye shall weep and lament, but the world shall rejoice: and ye shall be sorrowful, but your sorrow shall be turned into joy. 21 A woman when she is in travail hath sorrow, because her hour is come: but as soon as she is delivered of the child, she remembereth no more the anguish, for joy that a man is born into the world. 22 And ye now therefore have sorrow: but I will see you again, and your heart shall rejoice, and your joy no man taketh from you.

23 And in that day ye shall ask me nothing. Verily, verily, I say unto you, Whatsoever ye shall ask the Father in my name, he will give it you. 24 Hitherto have ye asked nothing in my name: ask, and ye shall receive, that your joy may be full. 25 These things have I spoken unto you in proverbs: but the time cometh, when I shall no more speak unto you in proverbs, but I shall shew you plainly of the Father. 26 At that day ye shall ask in my name: and I say not unto you, that I will pray the Father for you: 27 For the Father himself loveth you, because ye have loved me, and have believed that I came out from God.

28 I came forth from the Father, and am come into the world: again, I leave the world, and go to the Father. 29 His disciples said unto him, Lo, now speakest thou plainly, and speakest no proverb. Now are we sure that thou knowest all things, and needest not that any man should ask thee: by this we believe that thou camest forth from God. 31 Jesus answered them, Do ye now believe? 32 Behold, the hour cometh, yea, is now come, that ye shall be scattered, every man to his own, and shall leave me alone: and yet I am not alone, because the Father is with me. 33 These things I have spoken unto you, that in me ye might have peace. In the world ye shall have tribulation: but be of good cheer; I have overcome the world.

NOTES: JOHN CHAPTER 16

Discussion Point 4.19
Jesus' prayer for those whom he has called to be His Sons
In preparation for death, Jesus prays for his disciples and for those that believe on him that come through the work of the disciples. Note the specificity of the prayer. The prayer is first that God would glorify the Son as the Son glorifies him, Second, acknowledging that the Son has all power over flesh for the giving of eternal life to those whom the Father has called, and third, that the Father would return the Son to the glory that he had with the Father before the foundation of the world. Also note that Jesus proclaims that He has manifested God's name (Jesus) on earth. Finally, he prays, not for the world, but for those in the world, that God has called (John 17:1-26).

***

John Chapter 17

1 These words spake Jesus, and lifted up his eyes to heaven, and said, *Father, the hour is come; glorify thy Son, that thy Son also may glorify thee: 2 As thou hast given him power over all flesh, that he should give eternal life to as many as thou hast given him. 3 And this is life eternal, that they might know thee the only true God, and Jesus Christ, whom thou hast sent. 4 I have glorified thee on the earth: I have finished the work which thou gavest me to do. 5 And now, O Father, glorify thou me with thine own self with the glory which I had with thee before the world was. 6 I have manifested thy name unto the men which thou gavest me out of the world: thine they were, and thou gavest them me; and they have kept thy word. 7 Now they have known that all things whatsoever thou hast given me are of thee. 8 For I have given unto them the words which thou gavest me; and they have received them, and have known surely that I came out from thee, and they have believed that thou didst send me. 9 I pray for them: I pray not for the world, but for them which thou hast given me; for they are thine. 10 And all mine are thine, and thine are mine; and I am glorified in them.*

11 And now I am no more in the world, but these are in the world, and I come to thee. Holy Father, keep through thine own name those whom thou hast given me, that they may be one, as we are. 12 While I was with them in the world, I kept them in thy name: those that thou gavest me I have kept, and none of them is lost, but the son of perdition; that the scripture might be fulfilled. 13 And now come I to thee; and these things I speak in the world, that they might have my joy fulfilled in themselves. 14 I have given them thy word; and the world hath hated them, because they are not of the world, even as I am not of the world. 15 I pray not that thou shouldest take them out of the world, but that thou shouldest keep them from the evil. 16 They are not of the world, even as I am not of the world. 17 Sanctify them through thy truth: thy word is truth. 18 As thou hast sent me into the world, even so have I also sent them into the world. 19 And for their sakes I sanctify myself, that they also might be sanctified through the truth. 20 Neither pray I for these alone, but for them also which shall believe on me through their word; 21 That they all may be one; as thou, Father, art in me, and I in thee, that they also may be one in us: that the world may believe that thou hast sent me. 22 And the glory which thou gavest me I have given them; that they may be one, even as we are one: 23 I in them, and thou in me, that they may be made perfect in one; and that the world may know that thou hast sent me, and hast loved them, as thou hast loved me.

24 Father, I will that they also, whom thou hast given me, be with me where I am; that they may behold my glory, which thou hast given me: for thou lovedst me before the foundation of the world. 25 O righteous Father, the world hath not known thee: but I have known thee, and these have known that thou hast sent me. 26 And I have declared unto them thy name, and will declare it: that the love wherewith thou hast loved me may be in them, and I in them.

NOTES: JOHN CHAPTER 17

CHAPTER 5

God's Ultimate Sacrifice – Himself

In the previous Chapter, Jesus proclaimed on numerous occasions that He is the manna sent from heaven, that He is the fulfillment of the Old Testament Prophecies (see Chapter 3) of the coming of the Christ and that He and the Father are one. He proclaims that men shall honor the Son as they Honor the Father and that He has been given power for the forgiveness of sins, and for all judgment. Jesus also made it clear that no man comes to the Father except by Him. Here, Jesus is saying that acceptance of Jesus is the only way to receive salvation. To not accept Christ is to not accept God.

We also saw that when Peter declared his belief that Jesus was the Christ, Jesus affirmed that declaration, and that God the Father had revealed that truth to Peter, and that He would build His Church on Peter's profession of faith.

We also saw Jesus explain that He must die and rise again on the third day to meet the purpose for his manifest presence on earth. With this, He routinely admonished his disciples, demons whom He has cast out, and even many whom He healed, to restrain from publicizing that He was the Christ, so that the scriptures, and God's plan for His sacrifice and man's salvation could be implemented according to God's perfect will.

We also observed that Jesus made reference to him sending "The Holy Ghost." after his death and resurrection. Jesus referred to the Holy Ghost as the *Comforter*, who would glorify Jesus and the Father, and would remain after Jesus' death and resurrection within those who believe as their guide. Jesus proclaimed that blasphemy against the Holy Ghost shall not be forgiven.

Finally, we observed, that Jesus has instructed us to pray in His name, and in doing so, we are praying directly to the Father as He and the Father are one. This is why Christians start or end their prayers with "In Jesus' Name." As Jesus declared in his John 17 prayer, He has manifested God's name on earth, and upon completion of the work which He manifested himself on earth to do, He would return to the original glory that He had with the Father, before the earth was formed (*see Discussion Point 2.1 - Genesis 1:26-30*).

In this next chapter we will explore the death and resurrection of Christ toward the fulfillment of those scriptures.

Discussion Point 5.1
Jesus Declaration that the Wine of the Last Supper represents His blood, to be Shed for the Remission of Sins.
This declaration is at the center of God's plan for the salvation of mankind by sacrificing his earthly form for our sins, and is the basis for Holy Communion ceremonies practiced by Christians world-wide (Matt 26:26-28).

Discussion Point 5.2
Jesus Experiences Sadness and Sorrow as he Faced the Betrayal.
As Jesus prepared to be betrayed and put to death on the cross, His sorrow displays the significance of the sacrifice...that God subjected himself to human form to experience the fear, pain and suffering of the sacrifice for our sins. This was a perfect sacrifice, far more significant than sacrifices of ignorant and helpless goats and lambs as sin offerings of the Old Testament. Also note Jesus' first-hand understanding of the frailty of the human flesh as he witnessed Peter and the other disciples inability to remain awake during his prayer ("the spirit is willing but the flesh is weak"). God understands (not simply as an all-knowing distant observer, but as one who also experienced in human form) that we humans do not posses the strength to obey all of His commands. Therefore He understands with Godly understanding and human empathy, that He must forgive our failures (Matt: 26:36-46).

Discussion Point 5.3
Jesus' Silence when Faced with False Witnesses
Jesus, upon being falsely accused and questioned by the priest, holds his peace. When the priest asks Him if he is the Christ, Jesus replies "thou hast said" and proclaims that He will be seen on the right hand of power, and coming in the clouds of heaven (See Discussion Point 3.5 for Old Testament prophecies in Isaiah Chapter53 where Jesus silence was foretold – Matt. 26:57-68).

***

Matthew Chapter 26

1 And it came to pass, when Jesus had finished all these sayings, he said unto his disciples, 2 *Ye know that after two days is the feast of the passover, and the Son of man is betrayed to be crucified.* 3 Then assembled together the chief priests, and the scribes, and the elders of the people, unto the palace of the high

priest, who was called Caiaphas, *4* And consulted that they might take Jesus by subtilty, and kill him. *5* But they said, Not on the feast day, lest there be an uproar among the people. *6* Now when Jesus was in Bethany, in the house of Simon the leper, *7* There came unto him a woman having an alabaster box of very precious ointment, and poured it on his head, as he sat at meat. *8* But when his disciples saw it, they had indignation, saying, To what purpose is this waste? *9* For this ointment might have been sold for much, and given to the poor. *10* When Jesus understood it, he said unto them, *Why trouble ye the woman? for she hath wrought a good work upon me. 11 For ye have the poor always with you; but me ye have not always. 12 For in that she hath poured this ointment on my body, she did it for my burial. 13 Verily I say unto you, Wheresoever this gospel shall be preached in the whole world, there shall also this, that this woman hath done, be told for a memorial of her.* *14* Then one of the twelve, called Judas Iscariot, went unto the chief priests, *15* And said unto them, What will ye give me, and I will deliver him unto you? And they covenanted with him for thirty pieces of silver. *16* And from that time he sought opportunity to betray him.

17 Now the first day of the feast of unleavened bread the disciples came to Jesus, saying unto him, Where wilt thou that we prepare for thee to eat the passover? *18* And he said, *Go into the city to such a man, and say unto him, The Master saith, My time is at hand; I will keep the passover at thy house with my disciples.* *19* And the disciples did as Jesus had appointed them; and they made ready the passover. *20* Now when the even was come, he sat down with the twelve. *21* And as they did eat, he said, *Verily I say unto you, that one of you shall betray me.* *22* And they were exceeding sorrowful, and began every one of them to say unto him, Lord, is it I? *23* And he answered and said, *He that dippeth his hand with me in the dish, the same shall betray me. 24 The Son of man goeth as it is written of him: but woe unto that man by whom the Son of man is betrayed! it had been good for that man if he had not been born.* *25* Then Judas, which betrayed him, answered and said, Master, is it I? He said unto him, *Thou hast said.*

26 And as they were eating, Jesus took bread, and blessed it, and brake it, and gave it to the disciples, and said, *Take, eat; this is my body.* **27 And he took the cup, and gave thanks, and gave it to them, saying,** *Drink ye all of it;* **28** *For this is my blood of the new testament, which is shed for many for the remission of sins.*

HEALING PARALYSIS

29 But I say unto you, I will not drink henceforth of this fruit of the vine, until that day when I drink it new with you in my Father's kingdom. 30 And when they had sung an hymn, they went out into the mount of Olives. 31 Then saith Jesus unto them, All ye shall be offended because of me this night: for it is written, I will smite the shepherd, and the sheep of the flock shall be scattered abroad. 32 But after I am risen again, I will go before you into Galilee. 33 Peter answered and said unto him, Though all men shall be offended because of thee, yet will I never be offended. 34 Jesus said unto him, Verily I say unto thee, That this night, before the cock crow, thou shalt deny me thrice. 35 Peter said unto him, Though I should die with thee, yet will I not deny thee. Likewise also said all the disciples.

36 Then cometh Jesus with them unto a place called Gethsemane, and saith unto the disciples, *Sit ye here, while I go and pray yonder.* 37 And he took with him Peter and the two sons of Zebedee, and began to be sorrowful and very heavy. 38 Then saith he unto them, *My soul is exceeding sorrowful, even unto death: tarry ye here, and watch with me.* 39 And he went a little further, and fell on his face, and prayed, saying, *O my Father, if it be possible, let this cup pass from me: nevertheless not as I will, but as thou wilt.* 40 And he cometh unto the disciples, and findeth them asleep, and saith unto Peter, *What, could ye not watch with me one hour?* 41 *Watch and pray, that ye enter not into temptation: the spirit indeed is willing, but the flesh is weak.* 42 He went away again the second time, and prayed, saying, *O my Father, if this cup may not pass away from me, except I drink it, thy will be done.* 43 And he came and found them asleep again: for their eyes were heavy. 44 And he left them, and went away again, and prayed the third time, saying the same words. 45 Then cometh he to his disciples, and saith unto them, *Sleep on now, and take your rest: behold, the hour is at hand, and the Son of man is betrayed into the hands of sinners. 46 Rise, let us be going: behold, he is at hand that doth betray me.*

47 And while he yet spake, lo, Judas, one of the twelve, came, and with him a great multitude with swords and staves, from the chief priests and elders of the people. 48 Now he that betrayed him gave them a sign, saying, Whomsoever I shall kiss, that same is he: hold him fast. 49 And forthwith

he came to Jesus, and said, Hail, master; and kissed him. *50* And Jesus said unto him, *Friend, wherefore art thou come?* Then came they, and laid hands on Jesus, and took him. *51* And, behold, one of them which were with Jesus stretched out his hand, and drew his sword, and struck a servant of the high priest's, and smote off his ear. *52* Then said Jesus unto him, *Put up again thy sword into his place: for all they that take the sword shall perish with the sword. 53 Thinkest thou that I cannot now pray to my Father, and he shall presently give me more than twelve legions of angels? 54 But how then shall the scriptures be fulfilled, that thus it must be? 55 In that same hour said Jesus to the multitudes, Are ye come out as against a thief with swords and staves for to take me? I sat daily with you teaching in the temple, and ye laid no hold on me. 56 But all this was done, that the scriptures of the prophets might be fulfilled.* Then all the disciples forsook him, and fled.

57 And they that had laid hold on Jesus led him away to Caiaphas the high priest, where the scribes and the elders were assembled. *58* But Peter followed him afar off unto the high priest's palace, and went in, and sat with the servants, to see the end. *59* Now the chief priests, and elders, and all the council, sought false witness against Jesus, to put him to death; *60* But found none: yea, though many false witnesses came, yet found they none. At the last came two false witnesses, *61* And said, This fellow said, I am able to destroy the temple of God, and to build it in three days. *62* And the high priest arose, and said unto him, Answerest thou nothing? what is it which these witness against thee? *63* But Jesus held his peace. And the high priest answered and said unto him, I adjure thee by the living God, that thou tell us whether thou be the Christ, the Son of God. *64* Jesus saith unto him, *Thou hast said: nevertheless I say unto you, Hereafter shall ye see the Son of man sitting on the right hand of power, and coming in the clouds of heaven. 65* Then the high priest rent his clothes, saying, He hath spoken blasphemy; what further need have we of witnesses? behold, now ye have heard his blasphemy. *66* What think ye? They answered and said, He is guilty of death. *67* Then did they spit in his face, and buffeted him; and others smote him with the palms of their hands, *68* Saying, Prophesy unto us, thou Christ, Who is he that smote thee?

69 Now Peter sat without in the palace: and a damsel came unto him, saying, Thou also wast with Jesus of Galilee. 70 But he denied before them all, saying, I know not what thou sayest. 71 And when he was gone out into the porch, another maid saw him, and said unto them that were there, This fellow was also with Jesus of Nazareth. 72 And again he denied with an oath, I do not know the man. 73 And after a while came unto him they that stood by, and said to Peter, Surely thou also art one of them; for thy speech bewrayeth thee. 74 Then began he to curse and to swear, saying, I know not the man. And immediately the cock crew. 75 And Peter remembered the word of Jesus, which said unto him, *Before the cock crow, thou shalt deny me thrice.* And he went out, and wept bitterly.

NOTES: MATTHEW CHAPTER 26

HEALING PARALYSIS

Discussion Point 5.4
On the third day, the Angel of the Lord declares that Jesus has risen from the Tomb.
Following this, Jesus appeared to Mary Magdalene and instructed her to bring the disciples to Galilee to meet him (Matt 28:1-10).

Discussion Point 5.5
Jesus' Declaration that All Power is Given unto Me in Heaven and in Earth.
This declaration of "All Power" can not be taken lightly. Here, Jesus is without question declaring that He is God Himself, having the power and authority over All things. He is not a servant or messenger of God as were prophets who came before Him. He has the power to call men to judgment, to forgive sins, and to direct all activities in Heaven and on earth. He is the Creator, before the foundation of the world (see Discussion Point 2.1 - Genesis 1:26, Discussion Point 3.4 - Isaiah 9:6, Discussion Point 4.9 - Matthew 16:16, Discussion Point 4.15 - John 14:7, & Discussion Point 4.19 – John 17:5) manifest in human form. When we pray in His name, we are therefore praying to the Father (Matt 28:16-20).

***

Matthew Chapter 28

1 In the end of the sabbath, as it began to dawn toward the first day of the week, came Mary Magdalene and the other Mary to see the sepulchre. 2 And, behold, there was a great earthquake: for the angel of the Lord descended from heaven, and came and rolled back the stone from the door, and sat upon it. 3 His countenance was like lightning, and his raiment white as snow: 4 And for fear of him the keepers did shake, and became as dead men. 5 And the angel answered and said unto the women, Fear not ye: for I know that ye seek Jesus, which was crucified. 6 He is not here: for he is risen, as he said. Come, see the place where the Lord lay. 7 And go quickly, and tell his disciples that he is risen from the dead; and, behold, he goeth before you into Galilee; there shall ye see him: lo, I have told you. 8 And they

departed quickly from the sepulchre with fear and great joy; and did run to bring his disciples word. 9 And as they went to tell his disciples, behold, Jesus met them, saying, *All hail.* And they came and held him by the feet, and worshipped him. 10 Then said Jesus unto them, *Be not afraid: go tell my brethren that they go into Galilee, and there shall they see me.*

11 Now when they were going, behold, some of the watch came into the city, and shewed unto the chief priests all the things that were done. 12 And when they were assembled with the elders, and had taken counsel, they gave large money unto the soldiers, 13 Saying, Say ye, His disciples came by night, and stole him away while we slept. 14 And if this come to the governor's ears, we will persuade him, and secure you. 15 So they took the money, and did as they were taught: and this saying is commonly reported among the Jews until this day.

16 Then the eleven disciples went away into Galilee, into a mountain where Jesus had appointed them. 17 And when they saw him, they worshipped him: but some doubted. 18 And Jesus came and spake unto them, saying, *All power is given unto me in heaven and in earth. 19 Go ye therefore, and teach all nations, baptizing them in the name of the Father, and of the Son, and of the Holy Ghost: 20 Teaching them to observe all things whatsoever I have commanded you: and, lo, I am with you alway, even unto the end of the world.* Amen.

NOTES: MATTHEW CHAPTER 28

Discussion Point 5.6
Jesus Silence when Faced with False Accusations.
As prophesied in the Old Testament book of Isaiah (chapter 53), Jesus remained silent so that the prophecy could be fulfilled (Mark 15:1-5).

Discussion Point 5.7
Jesus' anguish upon Separation from God at the Point of Death
As Jesus died for our sins, note two important events. First, Jesus became temporarily separated from God the Father and reacts with anguish "My God my God, why hast thou forsaken me?" Secondly, and simultaneously with that death, the separation from God which was created when Adam committed that original sin, and which remained throughout the entire Old Testament, was repaired as "the veil of the temple was rent in twain from the top to the bottom." (Mark 15:34-38).

✳✳✳

Mark Chapter 15

1 And straightway in the morning the chief priests held a consultation with the elders and scribes and the whole council, and bound Jesus, and carried him away, and delivered him to Pilate. 2 And Pilate asked him, Art thou the King of the Jews? And he answering said unto him, *Thou sayest it.* 3 And the chief priests accused him of many things: but he answered nothing. 4 And Pilate asked him again, saying, Answerest thou nothing? behold how many things they witness against thee. 5 But Jesus yet answered nothing; so that Pilate marvelled.

6 Now at that feast he released unto them one prisoner, whomsoever they desired. 7 And there was one named Barabbas, which lay bound with them that had made insurrection with him, who had committed murder in the insurrection. 8 And the multitude crying aloud began to desire him to do as he had ever done unto them. 9 But Pilate answered them, saying, Will ye that I release unto you the King of the Jews? 10 For he knew that the chief priests had delivered him for envy. 11 But the chief priests moved the people, that he should rather release Barabbas unto them. 12 And Pi-

HEALING PARALYSIS

late answered and said again unto them, What will ye then that I shall do unto him whom ye call the King of the Jews? 13 And they cried out again, Crucify him. 14 Then Pilate said unto them, Why, what evil hath he done? And they cried out the more exceedingly, Crucify him.

15 And so Pilate, willing to content the people, released Barabbas unto them, and delivered Jesus, when he had scourged him, to be crucified. 16 And the soldiers led him away into the hall, called Praetorium; and they call together the whole band. 17 And they clothed him with purple, and platted a crown of thorns, and put it about his head, 18 And began to salute him, Hail, King of the Jews! 19 And they smote him on the head with a reed, and did spit upon him, and bowing their knees worshipped him. 20 And when they had mocked him, they took off the purple from him, and put his own clothes on him, and led him out to crucify him. 21 And they compel one Simon a Cyrenian, who passed by, coming out of the country, the father of Alexander and Rufus, to bear his cross. 22 And they bring him unto the place Golgotha, which is, being interpreted, The place of a skull. 23 And they gave him to drink wine mingled with myrrh: but he received it not. 24 And when they had crucified him, they parted his garments, casting lots upon them, what every man should take. 25 And it was the third hour, and they crucified him. 26 And the superscription of his accusation was written over, THE KING OF THE JEWS. 27 And with him they crucify two thieves; the one on his right hand, and the other on his left. 28 And the scripture was fulfilled, which saith, And he was numbered with the transgressors. 29 And they that passed by railed on him, wagging their heads, and saying, Ah, thou that destroyest the temple, and buildest it in three days, 30 Save thyself, and come down from the cross. 31 Likewise also the chief priests mocking said among themselves with the scribes, He saved others; himself he cannot save. 32 Let Christ the King of Israel descend now from the cross, that we may see and believe. And they that were crucified with him reviled him. 33 And when the sixth hour was come, there was darkness over the whole land until the ninth hour.

34 And at the ninth hour Jesus cried with a loud voice, saying, *Eloi, Eloi, lama sabachthani?* which is, being interpreted, *My God, my God, why hast thou forsaken me?* 35 And some of them that stood by, when they heard it, said, Behold, he calleth Elias. 36 And one ran and filled a spunge full of vinegar, and put it on a reed,

and gave him to drink, saying, Let alone; let us see whether Elias will come to take him down. *37* And Jesus cried with a loud voice, and gave up the ghost. *38* And the veil of the temple was rent in twain from the top to the bottom.

39 And when the centurion, which stood over against him, saw that he so cried out, and gave up the ghost, he said, Truly this man was the Son of God. *40* There were also women looking on afar off: among whom was Mary Magdalene, and Mary the mother of James the less and of Joses, and Salome; *41* (Who also, when he was in Galilee, followed him, and ministered unto him;) and many other women which came up with him unto Jerusalem. *42* And now when the even was come, because it was the preparation, that is, the day before the sabbath, *43* Joseph of Arimathaea, an honourable counsellor, which also waited for the kingdom of God, came, and went in boldly unto Pilate, and craved the body of Jesus. *44* And Pilate marvelled if he were already dead: and calling unto him the centurion, he asked him whether he had been any while dead. *45* And when he knew it of the centurion, he gave the body to Joseph. *46* And he bought fine linen, and took him down, and wrapped him in the linen, and laid him in a sepulchre which was hewn out of a rock, and rolled a stone unto the door of the sepulchre. *47* And Mary Magdalene and Mary the mother of Joses beheld where he was laid.

NOTES: MARK CHAPTER 15

Discussion Point 5.8
Jesus Raised from the Tomb on 3rd Day
He that believeth and is Baptized shall be saved, but he that believeth not shall be damned. See notes from Discussion Points 5.2 and 5.3 (Mark 16: 1-20).

※※※

Mark Chapter 16

1 And when the sabbath was past, Mary Magdalene, and Mary the mother of James, and Salome, had bought sweet spices, that they might come and anoint him. 2 And very early in the morning the first day of the week, they came unto the sepulchre at the rising of the sun. 3 And they said among themselves, Who shall roll us away the stone from the door of the sepulchre? 4 And when they looked, they saw that the stone was rolled away: for it was very great. 5 And entering into the sepulchre, they saw a young man sitting on the right side, clothed in a long white garment; and they were affrighted. 6 And he saith unto them, Be not affrighted: Ye seek Jesus of Nazareth, which was crucified: he is risen; he is not here: behold the place where they laid him. 7 But go your way, tell his disciples and Peter that he goeth before you into Galilee: there shall ye see him, as he said unto you. 8 And they went out quickly, and fled from the sepulchre; for they trembled and were amazed: neither said they any thing to any man; for they were afraid.
9 Now when Jesus was risen early the first day of the week, he appeared first to Mary Magdalene, out of whom he had cast seven devils. 10 And she went and told them that had been with him, as they mourned and wept. 11 And they, when they had heard that he was alive, and had been seen of her, believed not. 12 After that he appeared in another form unto two of them, as they walked, and went into the country. 13 And they went and told it unto the residue: neither believed they them.
14 Afterward he appeared unto the eleven as they sat at meat, and upbraided them with their unbelief and hardness of heart, because they believed not them which had seen him after he

HEALING PARALYSIS

was risen. *15 And he said unto them, Go ye into all the world, and preach the gospel to every creature. 16 He that believeth and is baptized shall be saved; but he that believeth not shall be damned. 17 And these signs shall follow them that believe; In my name shall they cast out devils; they shall speak with new tongues; 18 They shall take up serpents; and if they drink any deadly thing, it shall not hurt them; they shall lay hands on the sick, and they shall recover.*

19 So then after the Lord had spoken unto them, he was received up into heaven, and sat on the right hand of God. 20 And they went forth, and preached every where, the Lord working with them, and confirming the word with signs following. Amen.

NOTES: MARK CHAPTER 16

Discussion Point 5.9
Jesus Declares He Alpha and Omega and that He will judge all men according to their Works.
By doing His commandments men will have the right to the tree of life. And behold, I come quickly and my reward is with me, to give every man according as his work shall be. I am Alpha and Omega, the beginning and the end, the first and the last.
Blessed are they that do his commandments, that they may have right to the tree of life, and may enter in through the gates into the city. . .I Jesus have sent mine angel to testify unto you these things in the churches. I am the root and the offspring of David, and the bright morning star (Revelation 22:12-16).

Refer to Discussion Point 2.3 ~ Genesis 3:22

✵✵✵

Revelation Chapter 22

1 And he shewed me a pure river of water of life, clear as crystal, proceeding out of the throne of God and of the Lamb. 2 In the midst of the street of it, and on either side of the river, was there the tree of life, which bare twelve manner of fruits, and yielded her fruit every month: and the leaves of the tree were for the healing of the nations. 3 And there shall be no more curse: but the throne of God and of the Lamb shall be in it; and his servants shall serve him: 4 And they shall see his face; and his name shall be in their foreheads. 5 And there shall be no night there; and they need no candle, neither light of the sun; for the Lord God giveth them light: and they shall reign for ever and ever.

6 And he said unto me, These sayings are faithful and true: and the Lord God of the holy prophets sent his angel to shew unto his servants the things which must shortly be done. 7 *Behold, I come quickly:* blessed is he that keepeth the sayings of the prophecy of this book. 8 And I John saw these things, and heard them. And when I had heard and seen, I fell down to worship before the feet of the angel which shewed me these things. 9 Then saith he unto me, See thou do it not: for I am thy fellowservant, and of thy brethren the prophets, and of them which keep the sayings of this book: worship God. 10 And he saith unto me, Seal not the sayings of the prophecy of this book: for the time is at hand. 11 He that is unjust,

let him be unjust still: and he which is filthy, let him be filthy still: and he that is righteous, let him be righteous still: and he that is holy, let him be holy still.

12 And, behold, I come quickly; and my reward is with me, to give every man according as his work shall be. 13 I am Alpha and Omega, the beginning and the end, the first and the last. 14 Blessed are they that do his commandments, that they may have right to the tree of life, and may enter in through the gates into the city. 15 For without are dogs, and sorcerers, and whoremongers, and murderers, and idolaters, and whosoever loveth and maketh a lie. 16 I Jesus have sent mine angel to testify unto you these things in the churches. I am the root and the offspring of David, and the bright and morning star.

17 And the Spirit and the bride say, Come. And let him that heareth say, Come. And let him that is athirst come. And whosoever will, let him take the water of life freely. 18 For I testify unto every man that heareth the words of the prophecy of this book, If any man shall add unto these things, God shall add unto him the plagues that are written in this book: 19 And if any man shall take away from the words of the book of this prophecy, God shall take away his part out of the book of life, and out of the holy city, and from the things which are written in this book.

20 He which testifieth these things saith, *Surely I come quickly.* Amen. Even so, come, Lord Jesus. 21 The grace of our Lord Jesus Christ be with you all. Amen.

NOTES: REVELATION CHAPTER 22

CHAPTER 6

Jesus the Christ (According to Apostle Paul)

In the Previous Chapter, we explored the events that lead to the death and resurrection of Jesus. We noted that Jesus declared to the disciples during the last supper, that his body would be broken for man's sins, and that his blood would be shed for the remission of sins; the basis for the Christian celebration of Holy Communion.

We also witnessed Jesus intense sorrow as he prepared to sacrifice himself for our sins; a human emotion that God subjected himself to; one that imbues the significance of the sacrifice. As Jesus prepared to be sacrificed, He also experienced the failure of His closest supporters to remain awake as He prayed despite numerous requests. With this failure, Jesus proclaimed in a statement of human empathy, an understanding that the human flesh is weak, though intentions are good, and also recognized that His disciples would indeed turn away from Him in times of trouble. By God manifesting Himself on earth in human form, He experienced as a human, the frailties of being human, while yet being God.

God's sacrifice of himself was one of greater significance of any burnt offerings of animals identified in the Old Testament, and occurred exactly as foretold in the Old Testament prophesies. In obedience, Jesus subjected himself, though fully innocent, to the abuse, false accusations, suffering and ultimate death, as the perfect remedy for the single sin committed by Adam which condemned all of mankind to separation from God, hardship and death. While all powerful, and able to remove Himself from the cross, Jesus allowed the false accusations and bodily death to occur without defense, as a way to allow man to be reconciled with God, after the many centuries of separation and imperfect sacrifices following Adam's sin. As He died on the Cross, the veil separating man from God was torn.

After His death, Jesus was laid in a tomb, and on the third day, the Angel of the Lord appeared to Mary Magdalene, proclaiming that Jesus had risen from the dead and would re-appear to the disciples in Galilee, which He did. With His death and resurrection, Jesus declared that He has all power in Heaven and on earth, and instructed the disciples to go out and teach the good news of Him and baptizing those who believe in the name of the Father, Son and Holy Ghost. Those who believe would be saved, and those who did not believe would be damned. The Bible says that after this, Jesus was received up to heaven and sat on the right hand of the Father.

In this chapter, we will explore the teachings of the Apostle Paul, a former persecutor of Christians, chosen by Christ himself, to bear His name to the Gentiles, kings, and children of Israel (Acts 3:15).

Discussion Point 6.1
Paul Describes his Charge
He describes that he was commissioned "to make all men see what is the fellowship of the mystery which from the beginning of the world hath been hid in God, who created all things by Jesus Christ of whom the whole family in Heaven is named" (Ephesians 3:1-15).

✷✷✷

<u>Ephesians Chapter 3</u>

1 For this cause I Paul, the prisoner of Jesus Christ for you Gentiles, 2 If ye have heard of the dispensation of the grace of God which is given me to you-ward: 3 How that by revelation he made known unto me the mystery; (as I wrote afore in few words, 4 Whereby, when ye read, ye may understand my knowledge in the mystery of Christ) 5 Which in other ages was not made known unto the sons of men, as it is now revealed unto his holy apostles and prophets by the Spirit; 6 That the Gentiles should be fellowheirs, and of the same body, and partakers of his promise in Christ by the gospel: 7 Whereof I was made a minister, according to the gift of the grace of God given unto me by the effectual working of his power. 8 Unto me, who am less than the least of all saints, is this grace given, that I should preach among the Gentiles the unsearchable riches of Christ; 9 And to make all men see what is the fellowship of the mystery, which from the beginning of the world hath been hid in God, who created all things by Jesus Christ. 10 To the intent that now unto the principalities and powers in heavenly places might be known by the church the manifold wisdom of God, 11 According to the eternal purpose which he purposed in Christ Jesus our Lord: 12 In whom we have boldness and access with confidence by the faith of him. 13 Wherefore I desire that ye faint not at my tribulations for you, which is your glory. 14 For this cause I bow my knees unto the Father of our Lord Jesus Christ, 15 Of whom the whole family in heaven and earth is named,

16 That he would grant you, according to the riches of his glory, to

be strengthened with might by his Spirit in the inner man; *17* That Christ may dwell in your hearts by faith; that ye, being rooted and grounded in love, *18* May be able to comprehend with all saints what is the breadth, and length, and depth, and height; *19* And to know the love of Christ, which passeth knowledge, that ye might be filled with all the fulness of God. *20* Now unto him that is able to do exceeding abundantly above all that we ask or think, according to the power that worketh in us, *21* Unto him be glory in the church by Christ Jesus throughout all ages, world without end. Amen.

NOTES: EPHESIANS CHAPTER 3

Discussion Point 6.2
God Took on the Form of a Servant and Humbled Himself unto Death,
Jesus, who being in the form of God, thought it not robbery to be equal with God, But made himself no reputation, and took upon him the form of a servant and was made in the likeness of men, and being found in fashion as a man, he humbled himself and became obedient unto death, therefore God also hath highly exalted him, and given him a name which is above every name, That at the name of Jesus every knee should bow, of things in heaven and things under the earth, and that every tongue should confess that Jesus Christ is Lord to the glory of the Father (Philippians 2:5-11).

***

Philippians Chapter 2

1 If there be therefore any consolation in Christ, if any comfort of love, if any fellowship of the Spirit, if any bowels and mercies, *2* Fulfil ye my joy, that ye be likeminded, having the same love, being of one accord, of one mind. *3* Let nothing be done through strife or vainglory; but in lowliness of mind let each esteem other better than themselves. *4* Look not every man on his own things, but every man also on the things of others.

5 Let this mind be in you, which was also in Christ Jesus: *6* Who, being in the form of God, thought it not robbery to be equal with God: *7* But made himself of no reputation, and took upon him the form of a servant, and was made in the likeness of men: *8* And being found in fashion as a man, he humbled himself, and became obedient unto death, even the death of the cross. *9* Wherefore God also hath highly exalted him, and given him a name which is above every name: *10* That at the name of Jesus every knee should bow, of things in heaven, and things in earth, and things under the earth; *11* And that every tongue should confess that Jesus Christ is Lord, to the glory of God the Father.

12 Wherefore, my beloved, as ye have always obeyed, not as in my presence only, but now much more in my absence, work out your own salvation with fear and trembling. *13* For it is God which worketh in you

HEALING PARALYSIS

both to will and to do of his good pleasure. *14* Do all things without murmurings and disputings: *15* That ye may be blameless and harmless, the sons of God, without rebuke, in the midst of a crooked and perverse nation, among whom ye shine as lights in the world; *16* Holding forth the word of life; that I may rejoice in the day of Christ, that I have not run in vain, neither laboured in vain. *17* Yea, and if I be offered upon the sacrifice and service of your faith, I joy, and rejoice with you all. *18* For the same cause also do ye joy, and rejoice with me. *19* But I trust in the Lord Jesus to send Timotheus shortly unto you, that I also may be of good comfort, when I know your state. *20* For I have no man likeminded, who will naturally care for your state. *21* For all seek their own, not the things which are Jesus Christ's. *22* But ye know the proof of him, that, as a son with the father, he hath served with me in the gospel. *23* Him therefore I hope to send presently, so soon as I shall see how it will go with me. *24* But I trust in the Lord that I also myself shall come shortly. *25* Yet I supposed it necessary to send to you Epaphroditus, my brother, and companion in labour, and fellowsoldier, but your messenger, and he that ministered to my wants. *26* For he longed after you all, and was full of heaviness, because that ye had heard that he had been sick. *27* For indeed he was sick nigh unto death: but God had mercy on him; and not on him only, but on me also, lest I should have sorrow upon sorrow. *28* I sent him therefore the more carefully, that, when ye see him again, ye may rejoice, and that I may be the less sorrowful. *29* Receive him therefore in the Lord with all gladness; and hold such in reputation: *30* Because for the work of Christ he was nigh unto death, not regarding his life, to supply your lack of service toward me.

NOTES: PHILIPPIANS CHAPTER 2

Discussion Point 6.3
Give thanks to the Father by Jesus
And whatsoever ye do in word or deed, do all in the name of the Lord Jesus, giving thanks to God and the Father by him (Colossians 3:12-17).

***

Colossians Chapter 3

1 If ye then be risen with Christ, seek those things which are above, where Christ sitteth on the right hand of God. 2 Set your affection on things above, not on things on the earth. 3 For ye are dead, and your life is hid with Christ in God. 4 When Christ, who is our life, shall appear, then shall ye also appear with him in glory.

5 Mortify therefore your members which are upon the earth; fornication, uncleanness, inordinate affection, evil concupiscence, and covetousness, which is idolatry: 6 For which things' sake the wrath of God cometh on the children of disobedience: 7 In the which ye also walked some time, when ye lived in them.

8 But now ye also put off all these; anger, wrath, malice, blasphemy, filthy communication out of your mouth. 9 Lie not one to another, seeing that ye have put off the old man with his deeds; 10 And have put on the new man, which is renewed in knowledge after the image of him that created him: 11 Where there is neither Greek nor Jew, circumcision nor uncircumcision, Barbarian, Scythian, bond nor free: but Christ is all, and in all.

> 12 Put on therefore, as the elect of God, holy and beloved, bowels of mercies, kindness, humbleness of mind, meekness, longsuffering; 13 Forbearing one another, and forgiving one another, if any man have a quarrel against any: even as Christ forgave you, so also do ye. 14 And above all these things put on charity, which is the bond of perfectness. 15 And let the peace of God rule in your hearts, to the which also ye are called in one body; and be ye thankful. 16 Let the word of Christ dwell in you richly in all wisdom; teaching and admonishing one another in psalms and hymns and spiritual songs, singing

with grace in your hearts to the Lord. 17 And whatsoever ye do in word or deed, do all in the name of the Lord Jesus, giving thanks to God and the Father by him.

18 Wives, submit yourselves unto your own husbands, as it is fit in the Lord. 19 Husbands, love your wives, and be not bitter against them. 20 Children, obey your parents in all things: for this is well pleasing unto the Lord. 21 Fathers, provoke not your children to anger, lest they be discouraged. 22 Servants, obey in all things your masters according to the flesh; not with eyeservice, as menpleasers; but in singleness of heart, fearing God: 23 And whatsoever ye do, do it heartily, as to the Lord, and not unto men; 24 Knowing that of the Lord ye shall receive the reward of the inheritance: for ye serve the Lord Christ. 25 But he that doeth wrong shall receive for the wrong which he hath done: and there is no respect of persons.

NOTES: COLOSSIANS CHAPTER 3

Discussion Point 6.4
God was Manifest in the Flesh
God was manifest in the flesh, justified in the Spirit, seen of angels, preached unto the Gentiles, believed on in the world, received up into glory (1 Timothy 3:14-16).

***

<u>1 Timothy Chapter 3</u>

1 This is a true saying, If a man desire the office of a bishop, he desireth a good work. *2* A bishop then must be blameless, the husband of one wife, vigilant, sober, of good behaviour, given to hospitality, apt to teach; *3* Not given to wine, no striker, not greedy of filthy lucre; but patient, not a brawler, not covetous; *4* One that ruleth well his own house, having his children in subjection with all gravity; *5* (For if a man know not how to rule his own house, how shall he take care of the church of God?) *6* Not a novice, lest being lifted up with pride he fall into the condemnation of the devil. *7* Moreover he must have a good report of them which are without; lest he fall into reproach and the snare of the devil.

8 Likewise must the deacons be grave, not doubletongued, not given to much wine, not greedy of filthy lucre; *9* Holding the mystery of the faith in a pure conscience. *10* And let these also first be proved; then let them use the office of a deacon, being found blameless. *11* Even so must their wives be grave, not slanderers, sober, faithful in all things. *12* Let the deacons be the husbands of one wife, ruling their children and their own houses well. *13* For they that have used the office of a deacon well purchase to themselves a good degree, and great boldness in the faith which is in Christ Jesus.

> **14 These things write I unto thee, hoping to come unto thee shortly: 15 But if I tarry long, that thou mayest know how thou oughtest to behave thyself in the house of God, which is the church of the living God, the pillar and ground of the truth. 16 And without controversy great is the mystery of godliness: God was manifest in the flesh, justified in the Spirit, seen of angels, preached unto the Gentiles, believed on in the world, received up into glory.**

NOTES: 1 TIMOTHY 3

Discussion Point 6.5
God Made the world by Jesus, who God required all angels to worship.
God hath in these last days spoken unto us by His Son, whom he hath appointed heir of all things, by whom also he made the worlds: Who being the brightness of his glory, and the express image of his person, and the upholding if all things by the word of his power, when he had by himself purged our sins, sat down on the right hand of the Majesty on high, Being made so much better than the angels, as he hath by inheritance obtained a more excellent name than they (Hebrews 1:2-6).

※※※

Hebrews Chapter I

1 God, who at sundry times and in divers manners spake in time past unto the fathers by the prophets,

2 Hath in these last days spoken unto us by his Son, whom he hath appointed heir of all things, by whom also he made the worlds; 3 Who being the brightness of his glory, and the express image of his person, and upholding all things by the word of his power, when he had by himself purged our sins, sat down on the right hand of the Majesty on high; 4 Being made so much better than the angels, as he hath by inheritance obtained a more excellent name than they. 5 For unto which of the angels said he at any time, Thou art my Son, this day have I begotten thee? And again, I will be to him a Father, and he shall be to me a Son? 6 And again, when he bringeth in the firstbegotten into the world, he saith, And let all the angels of God worship him.

7 And of the angels he saith, Who maketh his angels spirits, and his ministers a flame of fire. 8 But unto the Son he saith, Thy throne, O God, is for ever and ever: a sceptre of righteousness is the sceptre of thy kingdom. 9 Thou hast loved righteousness, and hated iniquity; therefore God, even thy God, hath anointed thee with the oil of gladness above thy fellows. 10 And, Thou, Lord, in the beginning hast laid the foundation of the earth; and the heavens are the works of thine hands: 11 They shall

perish; but thou remainest; and they all shall wax old as doth a garment; *12* And as a vesture shalt thou fold them up, and they shall be changed: but thou art the same, and thy years shall not fail. *13* But to which of the angels said he at any time, Sit on my right hand, until I make thine enemies thy footstool? *14* Are they not all ministering spirits, sent forth to minister for them who shall be heirs of salvation?

NOTES: HEBREWS CHAPTER 1

CHAPTER 7

About Un-clean Meats

From the previous chapter we witnessed a few of the Apostle Paul's descriptions to the Gentiles of who Jesus was, and why He came. Notice the great continuity of what Paul says about Jesus, and what Jesus said about Himself.

Jesus, who was God himself and who created the world, manifest himself on earth, taking the form of a servant, sacrificed himself for our sins, that through his death we would have life everlasting. According to Paul, God the Father Himself referred to Jesus as God. God and Jesus are one.

Paul also instructed us (see Colossians 3), that as members of the body of Christ, we must expunge fornication, uncleanness, inordinate affection, idolatry, anger, wrath, filthy communication, and other earthly recrudescent practices which evoke the wrath of God. Though forgiven, practicing Christians must strive to free ourselves from the bondage that these and other earthly temptations present, as we learn to walk in Christ. This is where issues of character and self discipline under the guidance of the Holy Spirit can help us to become what God intends, to be more like God as we model ourselves after the human manifestation of God in Christ, and fulfill His purpose for each of us while on earth.

In this chapter we will address one of the other primary concerns that Muslims & Jews hold regarding Christians: *Do not defile your body by eating pork.*

Discussion Point 7.1
Before Adam's Sin God declared all Meats For Adam's Use
And God said, Behold, I have given you every herb bearing seed, which is upon the face of all the earth, and every tree, in the which is the fruit of a tree yielding seed; to you it shall be for meat. And to every beast of the earth, and to every fowl of the air, and to every thing that creepeth upon the earth, wherein there is life, I have given every green herb for meat: and it was so (Genesis 1:29-30).

***

Genesis Chapter 1

1 In the beginning God created the heaven and the earth. 2 And the earth was without form, and void; and darkness was upon the face of the deep. And the Spirit of God moved upon the face of the waters.

3 And God said, Let there be light: and there was light. 4 And God saw the light, that it was good: and God divided the light from the darkness. 5 And God called the light Day, and the darkness he called Night. And the evening and the morning were the first day.

6 And God said, Let there be a firmament in the midst of the waters, and let it divide the waters from the waters. 7 And God made the firmament, and divided the waters which were under the firmament from the waters which were above the firmament: and it was so. 8 And God called the firmament Heaven. And the evening and the morning were the second day.

9 And God said, Let the waters under the heaven be gathered together unto one place, and let the dry land appear: and it was so. 10 And God called the dry land Earth; and the gathering together of the waters called he Seas: and God saw that it was good. 11 And God said, Let the earth bring forth grass, the herb yielding seed, and the fruit tree yielding fruit after his kind, whose seed is in itself, upon the earth: and it was so. 12 And the earth brought forth grass, and herb yielding seed after his kind, and the tree yielding fruit, whose seed was in itself, after his kind: and God saw that it was good. 13 And the evening and the morning were the third day.

14 And God said, Let there be lights in the firmament of the heaven to divide the day from the night; and let them be for signs, and for seasons, and for days, and years: 15 And let them be for lights in the firmament of the heaven to give light upon the earth: and it was so. 16 And God made

two great lights; the greater light to rule the day, and the lesser light to rule the night: he made the stars also. 17 And God set them in the firmament of the heaven to give light upon the earth, 18 And to rule over the day and over the night, and to divide the light from the darkness: and God saw that it was good. 19 And the evening and the morning were the fourth day.

20 And God said, Let the waters bring forth abundantly the moving creature that hath life, and fowl that may fly above the earth in the open firmament of heaven. 21 And God created great whales, and every living creature that moveth, which the waters brought forth abundantly, after their kind, and every winged fowl after his kind: and God saw that it was good. 22 And God blessed them, saying, Be fruitful, and multiply, and fill the waters in the seas, and let fowl multiply in the earth. 23 And the evening and the morning were the fifth day.

24 And God said, Let the earth bring forth the living creature after his kind, cattle, and creeping thing, and beast of the earth after his kind: and it was so. 25 And God made the beast of the earth after his kind, and cattle after their kind, and every thing that creepeth upon the earth after his kind: and God saw that it was good.

26 And God said, Let us make man in our image, after our likeness: and let them have dominion over the fish of the sea, and over the fowl of the air, and over the cattle, and over all the earth, and over every creeping thing that creepeth upon the earth. 27 So God created man in his own image, in the image of God created he him; male and female created he them. 28 And God blessed them, and God said unto them, Be fruitful, and multiply, and replenish the earth, and subdue it: and have dominion over the fish of the sea, and over the fowl of the air, and over every living thing that moveth upon the earth.

29 And God said, Behold, I have given you every herb bearing seed, which is upon the face of all the earth, and every tree, in the which is the fruit of a tree yielding seed; to you it shall be for meat. 30 And to every beast of the earth, and to every fowl of the air, and to every thing that creepeth upon the earth, wherein there is life, I have given every green herb for meat: and it was so.

31 And God saw every thing that he had made, and, behold, it was very good. And the evening and the morning were the sixth day.

NOTES: GENESIS CHAPTER 1

HEALING PARALYSIS

Discussion Point 7.2
Sin Offering by the Priests to Bear the Iniquities of the Congregation was Not Sufficient
And Moses diligently sought the goat of the sin offering, and behold, it was burnt: and he was angry...saying, Wherefore have ye not eaten the sin offering in the holy place, seeing it is most holy, and God hath given it to you to bear the iniquity of the congregation, to make atonement for them before the Lord (Leviticus 10: 16-19)?

❊❊❊

Leviticus Chapter 10

1 And Nadab and Abihu, the sons of Aaron, took either of them his censer, and put fire therein, and put incense thereon, and offered strange fire before the LORD, which he commanded them not. 2 And there went out fire from the LORD, and devoured them, and they died before the LORD. 3 Then Moses said unto Aaron, This is it that the LORD spake, saying, I will be sanctified in them that come nigh me, and before all the people I will be glorified. And Aaron held his peace. 4 And Moses called Mishael and Elzaphan, the sons of Uzziel the uncle of Aaron, and said unto them, Come near, carry your brethren from before the sanctuary out of the camp. 5 So they went near, and carried them in their coats out of the camp; as Moses had said. 6 And Moses said unto Aaron, and unto Eleazar and unto Ithamar, his sons, Uncover not your heads, neither rend your clothes; lest ye die, and lest wrath come upon all the people: but let your brethren, the whole house of Israel, bewail the burning which the LORD hath kindled. 7 And ye shall not go out from the door of the tabernacle of the congregation, lest ye die: for the anointing oil of the LORD is upon you. And they did according to the word of Moses.

8 And the LORD spake unto Aaron, saying, 9 Do not drink wine nor strong drink, thou, nor thy sons with thee, when ye go into the tabernacle of the congregation, lest ye die: it shall be a statute for ever throughout your generations: 10 And that ye may put difference between holy and unholy, and between unclean and clean; 11 And that ye may teach the children of Israel all the statutes which the LORD hath spoken unto them by the hand of Moses. 12 And Moses spake unto Aaron, and unto Eleazar and unto Ithamar, his sons that were left, Take the meat offering that remaineth of

the offerings of the LORD made by fire, and eat it without leaven beside the altar: for it is most holy: *13* And ye shall eat it in the holy place, because it is thy due, and thy sons' due, of the sacrifices of the LORD made by fire: for so I am commanded. *14* And the wave breast and heave shoulder shall ye eat in a clean place; thou, and thy sons, and thy daughters with thee: for they be thy due, and thy sons' due, which are given out of the sacrifices of peace offerings of the children of Israel. *15* The heave shoulder and the wave breast shall they bring with the offerings made by fire of the fat, to wave it for a wave offering before the LORD; and it shall be thine, and thy sons' with thee, by a statute for ever; as the LORD hath commanded.

16 And Moses diligently sought the goat of the sin offering, and, behold, it was burnt: and he was angry with Eleazar and Ithamar, the sons of Aaron which were left alive, saying, *17* Wherefore have ye not eaten the sin offering in the holy place, seeing it is most holy, and God hath given it you to bear the iniquity of the congregation, to make atonement for them before the LORD? *18* Behold, the blood of it was not brought in within the holy place: ye should indeed have eaten it in the holy place, as I commanded. *19* And Aaron said unto Moses, Behold, this day have they offered their sin offering and their burnt offering before the LORD; and such things have befallen me: and if I had eaten the sin offering to day, should it have been accepted in the sight of the LORD?

20 And when Moses heard that, he was content.

NOTES: LEVITICUS CHAPTER 10

Discussion Point 7.3
The People Themselves must Set Aside Certain Foods as Sacrifice
And not simply rely on the actions and sacrifices of the priests for sin offerings. And the swine, though he divide the hoof, and be clovenfooted, yet he cheweth not the cud; he is unclean to you. (Leviticus 11:7-8)

Discussion Point 7.4
Sanctify Yourselves to be Holy as I am Holy
Here, God is telling the Jews that they must hold aside from consumption certain meats from the air, water and land regularly as a way of sanctifying themselves and remembering God's provision and protection (Leviticus 11:43-47).

***

Leviticus Chapter 11

1 And the LORD spake unto Moses and to Aaron, saying unto them, 2 Speak unto the children of Israel, saying, These are the beasts which ye shall eat among all the beasts that are on the earth. 3 Whatsoever parteth the hoof, and is clovenfooted, and cheweth the cud, among the beasts, that shall ye eat. 4 Nevertheless these shall ye not eat of them that chew the cud, or of them that divide the hoof: as the camel, because he cheweth the cud, but divideth not the hoof; he is unclean unto you. 5 And the coney, because he cheweth the cud, but divideth not the hoof; he is unclean unto you. 6 And the hare, because he cheweth the cud, but divideth not the hoof; he is unclean unto you.

> **7 And the swine, though he divide the hoof, and be clovenfooted, yet he cheweth not the cud; he is unclean to you. 8 Of their flesh shall ye not eat, and their carcase shall ye not touch; they are unclean to you.**

9 These shall ye eat of all that are in the waters: whatsoever hath fins and scales in the waters, in the seas, and in the rivers, them shall ye eat. 10 And all that have not fins and scales in the seas, and in the rivers, of all that move in the waters, and of any living thing which is in the waters, they shall be an abomination unto you: 11 They shall be even an abomination

unto you; ye shall not eat of their flesh, but ye shall have their carcases in abomination. *12* Whatsoever hath no fins nor scales in the waters, that shall be an abomination unto you. *13* And these are they which ye shall have in abomination among the fowls; they shall not be eaten, they are an abomination: the eagle, and the ossifrage, and the ospray, *14* And the vulture, and the kite after his kind; *15* Every raven after his kind; *16* And the owl, and the night hawk, and the cuckow, and the hawk after his kind, *17* And the little owl, and the cormorant, and the great owl, *18* And the swan, and the pelican, and the gier eagle, *19* And the stork, the heron after her kind, and the lapwing, and the bat.

20 All fowls that creep, going upon all four, shall be an abomination unto you. *21* Yet these may ye eat of every flying creeping thing that goeth upon all four, which have legs above their feet, to leap withal upon the earth; *22* Even these of them ye may eat; the locust after his kind, and the bald locust after his kind, and the beetle after his kind, and the grasshopper after his kind. *23* But all other flying creeping things, which have four feet, shall be an abomination unto you. *24* And for these ye shall be unclean: whosoever toucheth the carcase of them shall be unclean until the even. *25* And whosoever beareth ought of the carcase of them shall wash his clothes, and be unclean until the even. *26* The carcases of every beast which divideth the hoof, and is not clovenfooted, nor cheweth the cud, are unclean unto you: every one that toucheth them shall be unclean. *27* And whatsoever goeth upon his paws, among all manner of beasts that go on all four, those are unclean unto you: whoso toucheth their carcase shall be unclean until the even. *28* And he that beareth the carcase of them shall wash his clothes, and be unclean until the even: they are unclean unto you. *29* These also shall be unclean unto you among the creeping things that creep upon the earth; the weasel, and the mouse, and the tortoise after his kind, *30* And the ferret, and the chameleon, and the lizard, and the snail, and the mole. *31* These are unclean to you among all that creep: whosoever doth touch them, when they be dead, shall be unclean until the even. *32* And upon whatsoever any of them, when they are dead, doth fall, it shall be unclean; whether it be any vessel of wood, or raiment, or skin, or sack, whatsoever vessel it be, wherein any work is done, it must be put into water, and it shall be unclean until the even; so it shall be cleansed. *33* And every earthen vessel, whereinto any of them falleth, whatsoever is in it shall be unclean; and ye shall break it. *34* Of all meat which may be eaten, that on which such water cometh shall be unclean: and all drink that may be drunk in every such vessel shall be unclean. 35 And every thing whereupon any part of their carcase falleth shall be unclean; whether it be oven, or ranges for pots, they shall be broken down: for they are unclean, and shall be unclean unto you. 36 Nevertheless a fountain or pit, wherein there is plenty of water, shall be clean: but that which toucheth their carcase shall be unclean. 37 And if any part of their carcase fall upon any sowing seed which is to be sown, it shall be clean. 38 But if any water be put upon the seed, and any part of their carcase fall thereon, it shall be unclean unto you. 39 And if any beast, of which ye may eat, die; he that toucheth the carcase thereof shall be unclean until the even. 40 And he that eateth of the carcase of it shall wash his clothes, and be unclean until the even: he also that beareth the carcase of it shall wash his clothes, and be unclean until the even. 41 And every creeping thing that creepeth upon the earth shall be an abomination; it shall not be eaten. 42 Whatsoever goeth upon the belly, and whatsoever goeth upon all four, or whatsoever hath more feet among all creeping things that creep upon the earth, them ye shall not eat; for they are an abomination.

43 Ye shall not make yourselves abominable with any creeping thing that creepeth, neither shall ye make yourselves unclean with them, that ye should be defiled thereby. 44 For I am the LORD your God: ye shall therefore sanctify yourselves, and ye shall be holy; for I am holy: neither shall ye defile yourselves with any manner of creeping thing that creepeth upon the earth. 45 For I am the LORD that bringeth you up out of the land of Egypt, to be your God: ye shall therefore be holy, for I am holy. 46 This is the law of the beasts, and of the fowl, and of every living creature that moveth in the waters, and of every creature that creepeth upon the earth: 47 To make a difference between the unclean and the clean, and between the beast that may be eaten and the beast that may not be eaten.

NOTES: LEVITICUS CHAPTER 11

Discussion Point 7.5
Jesus Declares that Nothing From Outside the Man Can Defile Him
Hearken unto me every one of you and understand. There is nothing from without a man that entering into him can defile him: but the things which come out of him, those are they that defile the man... That which cometh out of the man, that defileth the man, for from within, out of the heart of men proceed evil thoughts, adulteries, fornications, murders, thefts, covetedness, wickedness, deceit... (Mark 7:9-23).

***

Mark Chapter 7

1 Then came together unto him the Pharisees, and certain of the scribes, which came from Jerusalem. 2 And when they saw some of his disciples eat bread with defiled, that is to say, with unwashen, hands, they found fault. 3 For the Pharisees, and all the Jews, except they wash their hands oft, eat not, holding the tradition of the elders. 4 And when they come from the market, except they wash, they eat not. And many other things there be, which they have received to hold, as the washing of cups, and pots, brasen vessels, and of tables. 5 Then the Pharisees and scribes asked him, Why walk not thy disciples according to the tradition of the elders, but eat bread with unwashen hands? 6 He answered and said unto them, *Well hath Esaias prophesied of you hypocrites, as it is written, This people honoureth me with their lips, but their heart is far from me. 7 Howbeit in vain do they worship me, teaching for doctrines the commandments of men. 8 For laying aside the commandment of God, ye hold the tradition of men, as the washing of pots and cups: and many other such like things ye do.*

9 And he said unto them, Full well ye reject the commandment of God, that ye may keep your own tradition. 10 For Moses said, Honour thy father and thy mother; and, Whoso curseth father or mother, let him die the death: 11 But ye say, If a man shall say to his father or mother, It is Corban, that is to say, a gift, by whatsoever thou mightest be profited by me; he shall be free. 12 And ye suffer him no more to do ought for his father or his mother; 13 Making the word of God of none effect through your tradition, which ye have delivered: and many such like things do ye. 14 And when he had

HEALING PARALYSIS

called all the people unto him, he said unto them, *Hearken unto me every one of you, and understand:* 15 *There is nothing from without a man, that entering into him can defile him: but the things which come out of him, those are they that defile the man.* 16 *If any man have ears to hear, let him hear.* 17 And when he was entered into the house from the people, his disciples asked him concerning the parable. 18 And he saith unto them, *Are ye so without understanding also? Do ye not perceive, that whatsoever thing from without entereth into the man, it cannot defile him;* 19 *Because it entereth not into his heart, but into the belly, and goeth out into the draught, purging all meats?* 20 And he said, *That which cometh out of the man, that defileth the man.* 21 *For from within, out of the heart of men, proceed evil thoughts, adulteries, fornications, murders,* 22 *Thefts, covetousness, wickedness, deceit, lasciviousness, an evil eye, blasphemy, pride, foolishness:* 23 *All these evil things come from within, and defile the man.*

24 And from thence he arose, and went into the borders of Tyre and Sidon, and entered into an house, and would have no man know it: but he could not be hid. 25 For a certain woman, whose young daughter had an unclean spirit, heard of him, and came and fell at his feet: 26 The woman was a Greek, a Syrophenician by nation; and she besought him that he would cast forth the devil out of her daughter. 27 But Jesus said unto her, *Let the children first be filled: for it is not meet to take the children's bread, and to cast it unto the dogs.* 28 And she answered and said unto him, Yes, Lord: yet the dogs under the table eat of the children's crumbs. 29 And he said unto her, *For this saying go thy way; the devil is gone out of thy daughter.* 30 And when she was come to her house, she found the devil gone out, and her daughter laid upon the bed.

31 And again, departing from the coasts of Tyre and Sidon, he came unto the sea of Galilee, through the midst of the coasts of Decapolis. 32 And they bring unto him one that was deaf, and had an impediment in his speech; and they beseech him to put his hand upon him. 33 And he took him aside from the multitude, and put his fingers into his ears, and he spit, and touched his tongue; 34 And looking up to heaven, he sighed, and saith unto him, *Ephphatha, that is, Be opened.* 35 And straightway his ears were opened, and the string of his tongue was loosed, and he spake plain. 36 And he charged them that they should tell no man: but the more he

charged them, so much the more a great deal they published it; 37 And were beyond measure astonished, saying, He hath done all things well: he maketh both the deaf to hear, and the dumb to speak.

NOTES: MARK CHAPTER 7

Discussion Point 7.6
What God Has Cleansed, That Call not thou Uncommon
Peter saw heaven opened and a certain vessel descending unto him as it had been a great sheet knit at the four corners and let down to the earth, wherein all manner of four-footed beasts of the earth and wild beasts and creeping things and fowls of the air...and there came a voice to him 'Rise Peter; kill and eat - But Peter said no Lord for I have never eaten any thing that is common of unclean, and the voice spake unto him again the second time "What God hath cleansed, that call not thou common" (Acts 10:9-16 Repeated in Acts 11).

✴✴✴

Acts Chapter 10

1 There was a certain man in Caesarea called Cornelius, a centurion of the band called the Italian band, *2* A devout man, and one that feared God with all his house, which gave much alms to the people, and prayed to God alway. *3* He saw in a vision evidently about the ninth hour of the day an angel of God coming in to him, and saying unto him, Cornelius. *4* And when he looked on him, he was afraid, and said, What is it, Lord? And he said unto him, Thy prayers and thine alms are come up for a memorial before God. *5* And now send men to Joppa, and call for one Simon, whose surname is Peter: *6* He lodgeth with one Simon a tanner, whose house is by the sea side: he shall tell thee what thou oughtest to do. *7* And when the angel which spake unto Cornelius was departed, he called two of his household servants, and a devout soldier of them that waited on him continually; *8* And when he had declared all these things unto them, he sent them to Joppa.

> **9** On the morrow, as they went on their journey, and drew nigh unto the city, Peter went up upon the housetop to pray about the sixth hour: **10** And he became very hungry, and would have eaten: but while they made ready, he fell into a trance, **11** And saw heaven opened, and a certain vessel descending unto him, as it had been a great sheet knit at the four corners, and let down to the earth: **12** Wherein were all manner of fourfooted beasts of the earth, and wild beasts, and creeping things, and fowls of the air. **13** And there came a voice to him, *Rise, Peter;*

kill, and eat. 14 But Peter said, Not so, Lord; for I have never eaten any thing that is common or unclean. 15 And the voice spake unto him again the second time, *What God hath cleansed, that call not thou common.* 16 This was done thrice: and the vessel was received up again into heaven.

17 Now while Peter doubted in himself what this vision which he had seen should mean, behold, the men which were sent from Cornelius had made enquiry for Simon's house, and stood before the gate, 18 And called, and asked whether Simon, which was surnamed Peter, were lodged there. 19 While Peter thought on the vision, the Spirit said unto him, Behold, three men seek thee. 20 Arise therefore, and get thee down, and go with them, doubting nothing: for I have sent them. 21 Then Peter went down to the men which were sent unto him from Cornelius; and said, Behold, I am he whom ye seek: what is the cause wherefore ye are come? 22 And they said, Cornelius the centurion, a just man, and one that feareth God, and of good report among all the nation of the Jews, was warned from God by an holy angel to send for thee into his house, and to hear words of thee. 23 Then called he them in, and lodged them. And on the morrow Peter went away with them, and certain brethren from Joppa accompanied him. 24 And the morrow after they entered into Caesarea. And Cornelius waited for them, and had called together his kinsmen and near friends. 25 And as Peter was coming in, Cornelius met him, and fell down at his feet, and worshipped him. 26 But Peter took him up, saying, Stand up; I myself also am a man. 27 And as he talked with him, he went in, and found many that were come together. 28 And he said unto them, Ye know how that it is an unlawful thing for a man that is a Jew to keep company, or come unto one of another nation; but God hath shewed me that I should not call any man common or unclean. 29 Therefore came I unto you without gainsaying, as soon as I was sent for: I ask therefore for what intent ye have sent for me? 30 And Cornelius said, Four days ago I was fasting until this hour; and at the ninth hour I prayed in my house, and, behold, a man stood before me in bright clothing, 31 And said, Cornelius, thy prayer is heard, and thine alms are had in remembrance in the sight of God. 32 Send therefore to Joppa, and call hither Simon, whose surname is Peter; he is lodged in the house of one Simon a tanner by the sea side: who, when he cometh, shall speak unto thee. 33 Immediately therefore I sent to thee; and thou hast well done that

thou art come. Now therefore are we all here present before God, to hear all things that are commanded thee of God.

34 Then Peter opened his mouth, and said, Of a truth I perceive that God is no respecter of persons: *35* But in every nation he that feareth him, and worketh righteousness, is accepted with him. *36* The word which God sent unto the children of Israel, preaching peace by Jesus Christ: (he is Lord of all:) *37* That word, I say, ye know, which was published throughout all Judaea, and began from Galilee, after the baptism which John preached; *38* How God anointed Jesus of Nazareth with the Holy Ghost and with power: who went about doing good, and healing all that were oppressed of the devil; for God was with him. *39* And we are witnesses of all things which he did both in the land of the Jews, and in Jerusalem; whom they slew and hanged on a tree: *40* Him God raised up the third day, and shewed him openly; *41* Not to all the people, but unto witnesses chosen before of God, even to us, who did eat and drink with him after he rose from the dead. *42* And he commanded us to preach unto the people, and to testify that it is he which was ordained of God to be the Judge of quick and dead. *43* To him give all the prophets witness, that through his name whosoever believeth in him shall receive remission of sins.

44 While Peter yet spake these words, the Holy Ghost fell on all them which heard the word. *45* And they of the circumcision which believed were astonished, as many as came with Peter, because that on the Gentiles also was poured out the gift of the Holy Ghost. *46* For they heard them speak with tongues, and magnify God. Then answered Peter, *47* Can any man forbid water, that these should not be baptized, which have received the Holy Ghost as well as we? *48* And he commanded them to be baptized in the name of the Lord. Then prayed they him to tarry certain days.

NOTES: ACTS CHAPTER 10

Discussion Point 7.7
Every Creature of God is Good if it is Received with Thanksgiving
Now the Spirit speaketh that, in the latter times some shall depart from the faith, giving heed to seducing spirits, and doctrines of devils; speaking lies in hypocrisy; having their conscience seared with a hot iron; Forbidding to marry, and commanding to abstain from meats, which God created to be received with thanksgiving of them which believe and know the truth. For every creature f God is good, and nothing to be refused, if is be received with thanksgiving (1 Timothy 4:1-5).

✳✳✳

1 Timothy Chapter 4

1 Now the Spirit speaketh expressly, that in the latter times some shall depart from the faith, giving heed to seducing spirits, and doctrines of devils; *2* Speaking lies in hypocrisy; having their conscience seared with a hot iron; *3* Forbidding to marry, and commanding to abstain from meats, which God hath created to be received with thanksgiving of them which believe and know the truth. *4* For every creature of God is good, and nothing to be refused, if it be received with thanksgiving: *5* For it is sanctified by the word of God and prayer.

6 If thou put the brethren in remembrance of these things, thou shalt be a good minister of Jesus Christ, nourished up in the words of faith and of good doctrine, whereunto thou hast attained. *7* But refuse profane and old wives' fables, and exercise thyself rather unto godliness. *8* For bodily exercise profiteth little: but godliness is profitable unto all things, having promise of the life that now is, and of that which is to come. *9* This is a faithful saying and worthy of all acceptation. *10* For therefore we both labour and suffer reproach, because we trust in the living God, who is the Saviour of all men, specially of those that believe. *11* These things command and teach. *12* Let no man despise thy youth; but be thou an example of the believers, in word, in conversation, in charity, in spirit, in faith, in purity. *13* Till I come, give attendance to reading, to exhortation, to doctrine. *14* Neglect not the gift that is in thee, which was given thee by prophecy, with the laying on of the hands of the presbytery. *15* Meditate upon these things; give thyself wholly to them; that thy profiting may appear to all. *16* Take heed unto thyself, and unto the doctrine; continue in them: for in doing this thou shalt both save thyself, and them that hear thee.

NOTES: I TIMOTHY CHAPTER 4

CHAPTER 8

Summary

In the previous chapter we explored the Old Testament and New Testament scriptures regarding clean and unclean meats. We saw that God created all meats to be eaten by Adam and Eve, prior to Satan's deception and Adam's original sin which separated Adam and the rest of mankind from God.

After God delivered the Jews from the hands of Pharaoh in Egypt, they became disobedient gluttonous idolaters consuming all that they desired. After God's required sin offerings were not being fully complied with by the Priests to bear the iniquity of the congregation, God commanded Moses to place significant restrictions on the consumption habits of the people, by declaring many beasts of the air, water and sea as "unclean to you" declaring that the people must sanctify themselves and be Holy as God is Holy. Notice how these dietary restrictions appear to be in direct conflict with God's original intention for Adam before sin and separation (Genesis 1:29), and remained in place throughout the entire approximate 2000 years between Moses and the birth of Jesus.

We then observed in the New Testament that Jesus, who declared that He came to fulfill, not destroy the law, reveals that nothing from without can defile a man; only that which comes out of his mouth and heart. He further informs Peter to "kill and eat" many of the beasts previously designated as unclean, with the rationale that "What God hath cleansed, that thou shall not call common." This indicates that God has cleansed those beasts restricted from the Jews as a sin offering. Finally, Paul, in his letter to Timothy declares that in latter times, some shall depart from the faith, presenting false doctrines from seducing spirits and devils that prevent marriage and eating of unclean meats, "which God created to be received with thanksgiving *by those who believe and know the truth.*"

Some may then ask, how (or when) did God cleanse those forbidden beasts?

If you've been paying attention over the course of this book, you can probably answer that question yourself, as well as deduce the logical rationale for it.

The death of the lamb, Jesus who willingly sacrificed himself for our sins, reconciled those whom God has called back to him. That sin offering; more perfect that goats and calves, as well as the restriction of foods of many kinds of meats (not just swine), is God's way of returning His sons and daughters to the everlasting life promised to Adam and Eve before Satan deceived us.

God did not "change his mind" and suddenly decide that it is now acceptable to eat swine. On the contrary, God sacrificed Himself so that the promise made to Adam and thereby all people called to be His sons and daughters could have everlasting life with Him. However, in order to have this eternal life, His children must seek him and reach for the tree of life (Genesis 3:22, Revelation 22:14).

Based upon the above, and the details described in Paul's letter to Timothy, all beasts can be eaten by those who believe and know the truth. Notice that Paul did not say that those beasts could be eaten by any and everyone...only for those who "believe and know the truth." (i.e. believe and know that Christ was God manifest on earth and sacrificed for our sins for our salvation). As described in I Timothy 4:5, these meats have been sanctified by the word of God and prayer (see Mark 7:15 and Acts 10:15).

Based upon this, it is my belief that that those who do not accept Christ should not consume these meats, as they remain under the old law of separation from God. As such, my family and I honor to this day, the dietary restrictions of those who do not eat pork. It is neither prepared nor served in our home. Not because it's not OK for us, not simply because my eating habits have not changed dramatically, and not solely out of respect for them. But rather because, according to my reading of the Bible it is not good for them... Not until they accept Christ - and I would not want them or myself to be on the penalty side of that law.

***

Accepting Christ is the only pathway to everlasting life. To not accept Christ, is to not accept God. Attempting to gain heaven via a series of rituals and deeds (no matter how well intentioned) will not get one into the Kingdom of Heaven. Such an approach; one which denies that Christ is God himself manifest on earth, born of a virgin, taking on the form of a human servant, experiencing the temptation and pain of the human body, witnessing the frailties of human flesh in the face of adversity with Godly understanding and human empathy, subjecting Himself to false accusation while silently presenting himself as a sacrifice for the sins of mankind, brutally put to death, descending to hell to pay for our sins, rising on the third day and returning to the original glory that He had with the Father in Heaven, and then sending a Comforter to be with us always; all so that we may be once again re-united with Him and have everlasting life as He promised to Adam; is folly. Christ is that "tree of life" that God proclaimed in Genesis 3:22 and Revelation 22:14 that we must take and eat of, in order to have everlasting life. To deny all of the above is not wise, and it is not prudent. To knowingly deny God and all that He is, is simply disobedient.

Beyond the necessity of accepting Christ to receive salvation or one's soul, I believe that we cannot fail to recognize the obvious benefits which we can receive under God's perfect will, while we occupy this human body, which comes with the acceptance of Christ.

Consider the mental and emotional freedom that one can learn to enjoy, as the gravity of the gift of knowing that you have eternal salvation of your soul (not hoping...but truly knowing and accepting it) begins to settle in. For some, the release of this level of uncertainty may be extraordinarily liberating, and may produce significant health benefits.

Imagine the comfort in knowing that you are the son or daughter, indeed part of the family of God Himself, and that even though you may err, He knows your needs and desires, and empathizes with the weakness of your flesh just as He empathized with the weakness of the flesh demonstrated by the disciples in the garden of Gethsemane immediately prior to his betrayal and arrest (see Matthew 26:40-41). Beyond the highest aspirations of any earthly Father, He wants you to have what you want, and has the power to appropriate it. If you know that within you, there exists an intentionality of congruence with God's desire for your life, and that by working to reduce the distracting power of the temptations which Paul described in Colossians 3, you are making room for God to mature your desires, and in so doing, that God will provide for those matured wants and needs at a level beyond your imagination. When we begin to allow the Holy Spirit to begin to guide us to align those matured wants and needs with our opportunities and resources, we may even improve economic liberty, as we no longer are enslaved by insatiable appetites or mountainous destructive debt, God willing.

Measure the value that comes with knowing that your Father (you are family now), has given you specific talents and strengths, not at random, but rather in accordance with the unique way that he designed you (see Matthew 25:14-30), to be used in accordance with His purpose, for you while on earth - after all, our purpose for living on earth is not simply to selfishly die and go to heaven, but rather to do His will. With practice and patience you will begin to know that putting that God-given talent to work in accordance with His will, under the leading of the Holy Spirit will be glorifying to Him, a blessing to those whom you serve, and profitable for you (*A.E. Fenton, un-published*). Though difficulties arise, you can have peace in your heart, and confidence that it is in God's hands, in accordance with His purpose.

Accept that all of the mistakes, bad choices, sins, and shortcomings of your past have been legally and contractually justified and pardoned, by reaching forth for the Tree of Life; by acceptance of Christ.

When I consider these and so many other blessings received not only in the after-life, but in these few days and years on earth, that come as a result of acceptance of Christ, I can not avoid thinking about the potential for extraordinary improvement in the health and well being of individuals, families, and communities which medical and public health professionals have been seeking for decades. Stress and anxiety mediated cardiovascular disease, stroke, hypertension, obesity, diabetes, gastrointestinal disorders, cancer, adolescent violence, substance abuse and other chronic health conditions are among the top causes of morbidity and mortality among American's and have been since the 1950's, despite an array of governmental, institutional and private sector administered health resource, health protection, and health promotion efforts. If we as individuals, families and communities could fully embrace the gifts and blessings that come along with this excellent salvation package, how much might we be able to attenuate the heavy toll of stress and lifestyle related ill health and premature loss of life that plagues this nation, and exacts such a heavy toll on our families and economy. Only God knows! For more information see *Healthy People 2000/2010* at *http://www.healthypeople.gov/*.

Not only are these chronic health conditions a significant problem for people throughout the entire nation, but African Americans experience these adverse health outcomes at rates significantly higher than those measured in the general population, for a variety of cultural, economic, and other factors, some of which have yet to be elucidated. All of this suggests that the potential health benefits of accepting Christ for African Americans at the individual, family or community level as related to the stress or anxiety mediated disorders mentioned above, as well as for the excesses in morbidity associated with violence and sexually transmitted diseases which plague youth and adolescents of this nation and African Americans in particular, may be especially promising. For more information on elevated rates of mortality and morbidity from chronic disease among African Americans, see "Covenant I - Securing the Right to Healthcare and Well-Being" within the recently released *Covenant with Black America*, Third World Press, and the Smiley Group, 2006.

Similarly, try to imagine the potential academic achievement benefits; (see Covenant II – Establishing a System of Public Education in Which all Children Achieve at High Levels and Reach their Full Potential) to students who have allowed Christ to shape their wants, goals and desires toward being truly excellent in their chosen fields of study. If these students, armed with the gift of the Holy Spirit, *"whom the Father will send in My name, teach you all things, and bring all things to your remembrance"* (John 14:16-25) can learn to ask the Holy Spirit for guidance as they interact with their teachers, peers and academic subject matter, how much better learning environments might public and private schools throughout America be? These same students, as they become adults could also learn to quietly invoke the name of Jesus to guide their decisions in the workplace, where the power of the Holy Spirit can guide them to improved ethical behaviors on the job, improved decision making, leadership and problem solving. How much of a Covenant VIII – "Accessing Good Jobs, Wealth and Economic Prosperity" opportunity potential exists simply from a decision to accept and grow in Christ? Again, God only knows!

Make no mistake about it. There are things that school districts, boards of education, state and federal governments must and should do to improve school environments and academic performance of students, and likewise, there are many things that must and should be done by politicians, governments and employers to improve economic opportunity and jobs for workers throughout this nation, but there are also things that we as individuals can and must do. Acceptance of Christ and learning to pray are among those individual things that we each must learn to do for ourselves, and it does matter. Of this I am sure.

For all of the reasons described above, as a public health professional, educator and entrepreneur, I believe that acceptance of Christ is one of the most important things that individuals can do toward improving health and well-being, academic achievement and economic independence. To my mind, any *Covenant* aimed at improving the health, social or economic conditions of a people - any people - is incomplete without acknowledging the importance of establishing a close relationship with God.

***

Final Remarks

In Chapter I there were seven key points of opposition to the acceptance of Christ which the scriptures highlighted in this book have addressed:

1. Does the Bible reveal that Christ is the Son of God? Answer – Yes,

HEALING PARALYSIS

Christ is the Son of God (see 2 Samuel 7:14-16, Isaiah 7:13-14, Isaiah 9:6-7, Matthew 16:16, John 3:16-17, John 17:2, Hebrews 1:2-5).

2. Is the worship of Christ, really worship of only a man or prophet? Answer – No, Christ is the manifestation of God himself in human form on earth via immaculate conception, to humble himself to experience our frailties and grief, and to bear and reconcile our sins so that we whom He calls back to Him might receive the salvation and everlasting life intended for all of mankind before Satan's deception of Adam (see Genesis 2:16-17, Isaiah 9:6-7, Matthew 7:21-23, Mathew 9:6, Matthew 16:19-28, Philippians 2:10-11).

3. If Jesus was really the earthly manifestation of God, then why didn't He simply openly declare it? Answer - So that God's perfect plan for his sacrifice, death, and descent to hell for the reconciliation of His sons could be fulfilled (see Genesis 3:14-15, Isaiah 53:1-9, Matthew 16:20-23, Mark 15:1-5, Mark 15:29-38, Philippians 2:7-8).

4. When we pray in Jesus' name, are Christians praying to the Creator himself or merely the creation? Answer - We are praying directly to the Creator because Jesus is the Creator, manifest on earth (see Isaiah 9:6-7, Matthew 28:18, John 6:35-51, John 14:6-7, John 14:13-14, John, 16:23-27, John 17:5-6, John 17:9-11, Ephesians 3:9-15, Colossians 3:17, Revelation 22:12-16).

5. Why do Christian's reference the Father, Son and Holy Ghost and is this "Trinity" Biblically justified? Answer - Jesus promised that after his sacrifice, death, resurrection and return to glory with the Father, that he would send a Comforter (Holy Ghost/Holy Spirit) to provide continued guidance and comfort to those whom have accepted him, and that The Holy Ghost would glorify Him (see Matthew 12:31-32, Matthew 28:19-20, John 14:15-18, John 16:7-15).

6. Does the Bible contradict itself with regard to who Jesus is? Answer: No – Jesus is Lord (see Isaiah 9:6, Matthew 16:16-17, Matthew 28:18, John 5:19-27, John 6:44-51, John 15:15-16, 1 Timothy 3:16).

7. Was the consumption of swine originally disallowed by God, and is it still Biblically wrong for Christians to consume this forbidden meat today? Answer – Before Satan's deception of Adam and Eve all meats and herbs were good, however after the deception and separation from God, and death of the part of God living within mankind, and the subsequent Old Testament inability of the priests to adequately make sacrifice offerings to bear the iniquity of the people, Moses, under God's direction declared many meats as "unclean to you" requiring that each person make a physical and behavioral sacrifice to sanctify themselves to be holy. In the New Testament, Jesus then declared that nothing that a person puts into their mouth can defile them, but rather that which comes out of their mouth can, and that He has cleansed those meats, for those who have accepted Him as that sacrifice. (See Genesis 1:29-30, Leviticus 10:16-17, Leviticus 11:7-8, Leviticus 11:43-44, Mark 7:9-15, Acts 10:14-15, I Timothy 1-5).

All of the above is subsumed in the first chapter of the Gospel of John; where the Bible states:

> "In the beginning was the Word, and the Word was with God, and the Word was God. The same was in the beginning with God. All things were made by him; and without him was not any thing made that was made. In him was life; and the life was the light of men. And the light shineth in darkness; and the darkness comprehended it not....That was the true Light, which lighteth every man that cometh into the world. He was in the world, and the world was made by him, and the world knew him not. He came unto his own, and his own received him not. But as many as received him, to them gave he power to become the sons of God, even to them that believe on his name: Which were born, not of blood, nor of the will of the flesh, nor of the will of man, but of God. And the Word was made flesh, and dwelt among us, (and we beheld his glory, the glory as of the only begotten of the Father,) full of grace and truth...And of his fullness have all we received, and grace for grace. For the law was given by Moses, but grace and truth came by Jesus Christ. No man hath seen God at

any time; the only begotten Son, which is in the bosom of the Father, he hath declared him" (John 1:1-18).

The paralyzed man described in the opening of this book, knew that he needed to find a way to get to Jesus, and as a result of his understood desire, and the with help of his trusted friends, his life in paralysis was healed. And it's like that with many of us. Nothing that you have done… and indeed nothing that you have failed to do, need deny you everlasting life with God. Find someone whom you can trust to help you understand who Jesus really is!

All that is then required for you to have the salvation that you so desperately seek, is to accept Him. Accept God in the fullest. By accepting Christ, you will not only gain eternal life, but you will also begin to reap the lifelong benefits of having a close relationship with your heavenly Father; a benefit that I thank God for daily.

Accepting Jesus is one of the most intelligent things that any of us can do!

I pray that the peace of God the Father, the Son, and the Holy Spirit will find its way into your mind, your heart, your soul, and into your life.

In Jesus' name, Amen.

SUMMARY NOTES

SUMMARY NOTES CONTINUED

BIOGRAPHY

Entrepreneur, university professor, health research scientist and author, Dr. Richard Lynch has spent the first 20 years of his career dedicated to improving the health and well being of people facing public health risks. He is routinely consulted by business leaders, government officials and attorneys in matters related to air quality, safety, workers compensation, and management, and is a noted public speaker on issues related to leadership, personal development, and business management practices. He serves on several scientific and policy advisory boards and is a dedicated husband and father of three, school board member, coach and member of Abundant Life Fellowship Church in Edgewater Park, NJ. Dr. Lynch holds a Ph.D. in Public Health from the Robert Wood Johnson Medical School/Rutgers University, and a Master of Science Degree in Industrial Hygiene from Temple University.

www.ingramcontent.com/pod-product-compliance
Lightning Source LLC
Chambersburg PA
CBHW060527100426
42743CB00009B/1455